BUILDING COMPETENCE IN SCHOOL CONSULTATION

School psychologists consistently indicate that consultation is a crucial component of their duties but that they lack sufficient opportunities to develop their corresponding knowledge, skills, and confidence during graduate training. *Building Competence in School Consultation* directly addresses the need for practical, comprehensive consultation training, including support materials, for school psychologists, counselors, and other professionals working in schools. Drawing from evidence-based approaches as well as experienced instructors' real-world toolkits, these essential perspectives and activities approach the standard and less common challenges of the school consultant role. Written by two leading experts in consultation, this book brings school psychology research directly to graduate students and both novice and experienced practitioners, providing invaluable context, reflection activities, videos from fellow consultation experts, and resources that translate academic findings into skills ready for immediate use.

Daniel S. Newman is Assistant Professor in the School Psychology Program at the University of Cincinnati, USA.

Sylvia A. Rosenfield is Professor Emerita at the University of Maryland, USA.

CONSULTATION, SUPERVISION, AND PROFESSIONAL LEARNING IN SCHOOL PSYCHOLOGY
Series Editor: Daniel S. Newman

Supervision in School Psychology
The Developmental, Ecological, Problem-solving Model
By Dennis J. Simon and Mark E. Swerdlik

Building Competence in School Consultation
A Developmental Approach
By Daniel S. Newman and Sylvia A. Rosenfield

CONSULTATION AND INTERVENTION IN SCHOOL PSYCHOLOGY
Series Editor: Sylvia A. Rosenfield

Consultee-Centered Consultation
Improving the Quality of Professional Services in Schools and Community Organizations
Edited by Nadine M. Lambert, Ingrid Hylander, and Jonathan H. Sandoval

Handbook of Multicultural School Psychology
An Interdisciplinary Perspective
Edited by Giselle B. Esquivel, Emilia C. Lopez, and Sara G. Nahari

Handbook of Research in School Consultation
Edited by William P. Erchul and Susan M. Sheridan

Becoming a School Consultant
Lessons Learned
Edited by Sylvia A. Rosenfield

Crisis Counseling, Intervention and Prevention in the Schools, Third Edition
Edited by Jonathan H. Sandoval

An Introduction to Consultee-Centered Consultation in the Schools
By Jonathan H. Sandoval

Handbook of Research in School Consultation, Second Edition
Edited by William P. Erchul and Susan M. Sheridan

Consultation Across Cultural Contexts
Consultee-Centered Case Studies
Edited by Antoinette Halsell Miranda

International Handbook of Consultation in Educational Settings
Edited by Chryse Hatzichristou and Sylvia A. Rosenfield

Handbook of Multicultural School Psychology
An Interdisciplinary Perspective, Second Edition
Edited by Emilia C. Lopez, Sara G. Nahari, and Sherrie L. Proctor

For more information about this series, please visit: https://www.routledge.com/Consultation-Supervision-and-Professional-Learning-in-School-Psychology-Series/book-series/CSAPLISPS.

BUILDING COMPETENCE IN SCHOOL CONSULTATION

A Developmental Approach

Daniel S. Newman and Sylvia A. Rosenfield

Routledge
Taylor & Francis Group

NEW YORK AND LONDON

First published 2019
by Routledge
711 Third Avenue, New York, NY 10017

and by Routledge
2 Park Square, Milton Park, Abingdon, Oxon, OX14 4RN

Routledge is an imprint of the Taylor & Francis Group, an informa business

© 2019 Taylor & Francis

Library of Congress Cataloging-in-Publication Data
A catalog record for this title has been requested

ISBN: 978-1-138-02261-4 (hbk)
ISBN: 978-1-138-02262-1 (pbk)
ISBN: 978-1-315-77697-2 (ebk)

Typeset in Bembo
by Deanta Global Publishing Services, Chennai, India

Visit the eResources: www.routledge.com/9781138022621

CONTENTS

TABLES

ACTIVITIES

PREFACE

We're not saying it's easy. We're saying it's worth it.

Consultation is a core skill for school psychologists and other professionals working in schools. As with every skill, consultation requires professional training. In this book we hope to provide a basic set of principles and activities for developing your skills as a school consultant based on our combined experience of over five decades of practicing, teaching, and researching consultation. Our goal is to make a difference in the quality of school consultation training provided to school psychologists, as well as school counselors and others who will enact the consultant role in schools, by supporting the development of self-efficacy and competence to provide effective consultation services. We hope also that this text will be a support to university-trainers' and field supervisors' self-efficacy and competence to instruct and supervise consultation.

In training professionals, some approaches to training are considered more effective than others. Best practice in learning to be a school consultant has been of interest for decades. In 1980, the National Conference on Consultation Training (Alpert & Meyers, 1983), supported by APA and multiple divisions of APA, was held at McGill University in Canada. Most of the topics discussed at the Conference continue to be relevant to consultation training today, including: (a) understanding the context/system within which consultation will be done, (b) recognizing the importance of consultation processes, and (c) building skills for successfully conducting the processes. However, evidence has existed for decades demonstrating gaps in the quality and quantity of consultation training provided to school psychologists at the pre-service level, including (a) limited coursework (i.e., too many programs provide only one course), (b) few supervision supports, and (c) limited attention given to complex processes such as building relationships or cross-cultural consultation (see Anton-LaHart & Rosenfield, 2004; Hazel, Laviolette, & Lineman, 2010; Hazel, Newman, & Barrett, 2016; Newman, Barrett, & Hazel, 2015).

It is counterintuitive to expect individuals to consult effectively when they do not have sufficient opportunities to develop the knowledge, skills, or confidence to do so at the pre-service level. School psychologist practitioners have consistently reported spending limited time engaged in school consultation (e.g., Castillo, Curtis, & Gelley, 2012). It is not as if school psychologists do not want to consult; they consistently indicate that consultation is a preferred role (e.g., Guiney, Harris, Zusho, & Cancelli, 2014; Hosp & Reschly, 2002). However, in a recent survey of NASP members, participants reported spending approximately 10% of their time in individual consultation, and 6% in systems-level consultation activities, with the majority of their time devoted to special education related activities (Castillo et al., 2012).

Lack of skills, including skill in entering the school culture as a consultant, remains a critical reason why school psychologists are not engaging in more consultation practice. If consultation is to be considered a pivotal clinical skill, like other clinical skills (e.g., assessment, counseling), opportunities for practice and feedback through coaching or supervision at the preservice, as well as the in-service, level, are needed to develop competence, proficiency, and eventually expertise over time (Harvey & Struzziero, 2008; Rosenfield, Levinsohn-Klyap, & Cramer, 2010).

In this book, we hope to bring you methods and activities that have engaged and prepared school consultants to work both at a systems level and an individual consultee level. This is a relatively short book, but don't be misled—it is filled with activities for you to develop your thinking and skills. If you simply read through without doing the activities, you will miss the opportunity to make the most of this book. To make it easier to complete the book's activities, printable online versions of all activities can be found on the book's webpage at the following URL: www.routledge.com/9781138022621. Some of the activities are to be completed individually, and some with a partner or small group. The variety of activities will enable individual readers (including those instructing, supervising, as well as those learning consultation) to pinpoint content to best match their needs at a given point in time. No matter your role, we hope that you will consider keeping this book and revisiting the content and the activities in the future to continue your consultation learning process.

Practice with feedback and supervision is the road to competence in every professional domain. As you learn and practice the skills and concepts provided in this book, they will come alive if you also are spending time in a school where you can observe how the school works as an organization (i.e., its culture, structure, and staff) and have the opportunity to engage with a teacher in a consultation experience. We don't expect that every experience in which you participate will be successful, and we do know that many will challenge you.

The activities in this book will also involve a great deal of reflection and deliberate practice on your part. We anticipate that you will need to record your interactions to be more aware of your verbal and non-verbal behavior—we have found many times that novice consultants are not aware of the words and content of their interactions with teachers. A response in supervision that we have heard often is, "*did I really say that?*" Also, there is need for coaching and supervision of your work to provide you with invaluable feedback. When we don't know what we don't know, it is easy to make unknowing errors in content and process, and worse yet, to have those errors become comfortable and repeated over time. We strongly believe in constant personal reflection as well as feedback from more experienced consultants.

Our hope is that through this work, you come to see consultation as a crucial component of your school practice. And, that in learning the skills here, you will become so much more comfortable and confident with the process that you will use consultation in your practice in the schools.

ACKNOWLEDGMENTS

We wish to acknowledge all the students we have taught at Fordham University, Temple University, the University of Maryland, National Louis University, and the University of Cincinnati. Without their feedback and participation, this book could not have been written, or perhaps not written in the way we have constructed it. In fact, all of the transcripts are real dialogues or reflections from students, although of course identifying features have been removed, and each excerpt is representative of multiple similar cases.

Thank you to Hallie Fetterman, a talented school psychology doctoral student at the University of Cincinnati, for providing helpful feedback and logistical support on this book. Thanks as well to Jud Phay (JP) Leong, Multimedia Coordinator, and his team in the College of Education, Criminal Justice, and Human Services at the University of Cincinnati for helping coordinate and edit the book's video resources. Our thanks also to many colleagues who over time have participated with us in research and extended conversations about training. Daniel would like to thank his current colleagues at the University of Cincinnati: Tai Collins, Janet Graden, Renee Hawkins, and Julie Morrison, for being wonderful collaborators and models of school psychology training. Sylvia would like to extend appreciation and thanks to Todd Gravois for his incredible influence on this book through his work in co-constructing the IC Team model, in developing the highest implementation standards for the work, and partnering in our joint research together over so many years. So many others in the schools and in the Lab for IC Teams have also contributed to my thinking and the way in which this book has been written—thank you.

We are grateful for the support of Daniel Schwartz, Editor at Routledge, for believing in this project and supporting its development. Thanks as well to our past editors with whom we have worked toward this point: Lane Akers and Rebecca Novack.

Finally, we would like to thank the consultation experts who contributed a video or other materials to this book: Lauren Kaiser (Millersville University), Antoinette Miranda (Ohio State University), Katurah Cramer (Howard County Public Schools), Colette Ingraham (San Diego State University), Janet Graden, Amanda Covey, Keisha Hill, and Julie Smith (University of Cincinnati), Elise Pas (Johns Hopkins University), Arlene Silva (William James College), Markeda Newell, and David Shriberg (Loyola University Chicago). We are grateful that you have been willing to share your wisdom with the readers.

1

CONSULTATION TRAINING

Making It Work

Everything starts somewhere.

(Terry Pratchett, Hogfather)

One of the critical domains of school psychology practice is consultation. Our purpose here is to provide you with the beginning knowledge, attitudes, and skills to enter the profession able to engage in consultation. But consultation is a term with many meanings. So how is school consultation defined?

A good place to begin is to examine what your current perception of school consultation is as a part of your role. First, consider your own personal image of a consultant in the schools.

ACTIVITY 1.1 (INDIVIDUAL)

Warm-Up Questions: Introduction

Write down your own assumptions regarding what you consider to be the role of the consultant in the school setting. You can write sentences or just key words.

1. What do you think a consultant does?
2. How does the role of consultant fit into your own image of the role of a school psychologist or school counselor?

(To make it easier to complete the book's activities, printable online versions of all activities can be found on the book's webpage at the following URL: www.routledge.com/9781138022621.)

Now that you have thought about your own assumptions, we will share ours. We begin this text with two key assumptions:

> **Assumption 1:** Consultation is a *pivotal clinical skill* for school psychologists. There is no other skill more foundational than consultation (Ysseldyke et al., 2006). Indeed, consultation is considered by the American Psychological Association (APA) to be one of six foundational competencies required for all psychologists (Fouad et al., 2009), and by the National Association of School Psychologists as a core domain in training and practice (NASP, 2010b). Further, it is rare for any assessments or interventions to occur without consultation, as the interactions leading to those decisions happen within a social context: "Someone must decide that an intervention is needed. Someone must select an intervention ... Finally, someone must determine whether the intervention has been successful and make adjustments ... and determine follow-up ... adding a consultant layer ... is a straightforward notion" (VanDerHeyden, 2014, p. 140).

> **Assumption 2:** As with other clinical skills, to develop *competency* in consultation requires adequate content knowledge as well as sufficient opportunities for distributed practice over time, supported by developmentally appropriate supervision. The assumption that psychologists prepared for direct service are also prepared for indirect service has been rightfully challenged (Gutkin & Conoley, 1990). We support the caution that without appropriate training, consultants risk causing harm to consultees and clients, based on action or lack of action in a case (O'Roark, 2002).

Being a school consultant is an enormous responsibility. Consultants have the potential to impact individuals directly (e.g., teachers, administrators, parents) and indirectly (e.g., students) as well as to influence systems (e.g., classrooms, teams, schools, and even school districts). However, we can't expect consultants-in-training (CITs) to consult effectively in *real life* if they do not have sufficient opportunities to practice these skills with a safety net; if they do not receive meaningful feedback via supervision; or if they do not know what they do not know. This assumption raises the question that is at the heart and purpose of this text: How can we build competence in consultation?

Why Assumptions Are Important

These assumptions may not seem particularly controversial to you. However, we do not believe that the majority of trainees, practitioners, or graduate educators consistently share these assumptions, or that they are regularly reflected in actual consultation training or practice. In short, there is a tension between the purported value of consultation in school psychology and how consultation training and practice ensues in graduate training programs and in the field. As a result of reading this book, we hope you come to view consultation as (a) a distinct competency area that is complex yet well-defined; (b) teachable and learnable with the proper tools and support; and (c) worth the effort to teach, supervise, learn, and practice given the potential benefits that result for consultants, consultees (e.g., teachers, parents), clients (e.g., students), and systems (e.g., schools, districts).

To begin, let us consider in more detail what school consultation is and how it is implemented in contemporary school settings. Imagine you are approached by a teacher in the hallway who shares a concern and then asks, "What should I do?" On first thought, it might seem simpler or more efficient to tell the teacher what to do rather than to schedule a time to explore problems and solutions in greater depth. Yet when the teacher does not do what you suggested, when the problem persists, when the student gets an inappropriate referral to special education, or when the implemented intervention clearly does not match with the problem, you may wind up asking yourself, "Was this really a more efficient way to consult?" To answer this question, it is helpful for us to define school consultation more specifically.

School Consultation Defined

We know that consultation means different things to different people. It may even be devoid of meaning altogether for some, given the wide variety of contexts, relationships, and actions which consultation may describe. Here we present definitions of school consultation that we will tie in later in the chapter to our core model of School Consultation.

To a layperson, consultation is "meeting with someone to talk about a problem," a definition that is accurate but obviously oversimplified. How each component of the layperson's definition (i.e., meeting; someone; to talk; problem) is elaborated likely diverges based on one's view of consultation training and practice. Such a broad definition also fails to differentiate between consultation and related areas such as counseling or therapy, coaching, supervision, mentoring, and teaching.

Consultation is *not* supervision, nor is it coaching, counseling/therapy, mentoring, or teaching. Although each of these services share several commonalities, and all are interpersonal processes to provide support, they are in several ways unique (see Table 1.1). In the sections that follow, we highlight distinct features of consultation, beginning with a definition.

Zins and Erchul (2002) provided a well-articulated definition of school consultation that links with practices considered hallmarks of competent practice:

> School consultation is defined as a method of providing preventively oriented psychological and educational services in which consultants and consultees form cooperative partnerships and engage in a reciprocal, systematic problem-solving process guided by ecobehavioral principles. The goal is to enhance and empower consultee systems, thereby promoting students' well-being and performance.
>
> *(p. 626)*

TABLE 1.1 Comparison of Features of Consultation and Related Services

Definitional Feature	Consultation	Type of Service				
		Counseling/Therapy	Coaching	Supervision	Mentoring	Teaching
Hierarchical	N	Y	Y	Y	S	Y
Evaluative	N	N	S	Y	Y	Y
Ongoing	S	Y	Y	Y	Y	Y
Confidential	S	Y	S	Y	S	N
Voluntary participation	Y	Y	S	N	Y	N
Choice of partner	Y	Y	S	N	Y	N
Guided by a priori content/curricula	N	N	S	N	N	Y
Gatekeeping function	N	N	N	Y	N	Y
Addresses professional problems	Y	S	Y	Y	Y	N
Addresses personal problems	N	Y	N	N	S	N
Involves professional learning	Y	N	Y	Y	Y	Y

Note: Y = Yes; N = No; S = Sometimes.

First of all, the definition refers to consultation as a *preventative orientation* or framework. Consultation is inherently linked to primary prevention, risk reduction, early intervention, and treatment efforts (see Meyers & Nastasi, 1999; Meyers, Meyers, & Grogg, 2004). In addition, consultation can support a salutogenic approach, which focuses on promoting health and well-being, rather than only preventing problems (Hylander, 2017). School consultants aim to *empower* teachers, administrators, and other consultees with the knowledge and skills not only to tackle the problem at hand, but also to learn from the process and apply new skills to prevent problems from occurring in the future, as well as to sustain healthy and thriving students (Hylander, 2017; Rosenfield, 2014; Sandoval, 2014).

Consultation is typically considered a method of *indirect service delivery* in which the consultee ultimately maintains problem ownership. Although consultants may have some role in intervention delivery, the primary responsibility for intervention implementation usually lies with the consultee. This speaks to the need for consultees to maintain as much as possible a sense of ownership over the problem and solution during the consultation process. Both consultants and consultees keep an eye on promoting positive academic, behavioral, and social-emotional outcomes for students; however, the consultant also maintains a focus on promoting positive consultee outcomes at the forefront of his or her efforts.

Within the *cooperative partnership*, "consultants structure and guide the overall process, while consultees supply much of the content of the discussion" (Zins & Erchul, 2002, p. 627), since it is the consultee who brings the problem to the process. The relationship is one of equals, with the parties bringing divergent knowledge to the table, and taking on different mutually agreed upon responsibilities during a *systematic problem-solving process*, with clearly defined stages. The relationship includes *reciprocal interactions*, where consultants and consultees both may change their conceptions of the problem along the way (Hylander, 2012). Consultees have a story to tell, and change is the evolution of a new story. For example, a teacher may experience a *turning* where she begins to view a student as lacking sufficient prior knowledge to be successful in the curriculum in contrast to her initial perception of the student as *disabled* or *lazy*. This new frame may be considered *ecological* or *ecobehavioral*, in that the dyad moves away from defining the problem in language that focuses on student deficits in isolation, but rather on the student's strengths and needs within a larger context (e.g., in schools, an instructional environment including task demands and instructional supports).

Novice, Routine, and Competent Consultation

For school-based practitioners to embrace this model in their work, it is essential that they have the skills required. There are different levels of competence in the development of consultation skill and practice. In what we subsequently define as novice consultation, routine consultation, and competent consultation, the components of a layperson's definition of consultation are elaborated differently (see Table 1.2).

TABLE 1.2 Differences in Understanding and Application of Consultation: Novice, Routine, and Competent Consultation

Component of Layperson Definition	Novice Consultation	Routine Consultation	Competent Consultation
Meeting	• Brief • Mostly one-time • Mostly "On-the-fly" • Any location (e.g., in the hallway)	• Brief • Mostly one-time • Mostly "On-the-fly" • Any location (e.g., in the hallway)	• Sufficient time for problem-solving • Mostly ongoing • Mostly pre-scheduled • Contract to establish meeting times, structure, and process for consultation • Quiet location free from interruptions
Someone	• One teacher • Parent • Focus on personal relationship with consultee	• One teacher • Parent • Administrator • Teams (grade-level; multidisciplinary) • Focus on professional relationship with consultee(s)	• One teacher • Parent • Administrator • Teams (grade-level; multidisciplinary) • Focus on professional relationship with consultee(s)
To Talk	• Lack of communication skill awareness/viewed as "common sense" or awareness of skills but rigid application • Ask relevant questions directing conversation towards own problem conceptualization • Offer information/advice/solutions before active listening	• Lack of communication skill awareness/viewed as "common sense" • Ask relevant questions directing conversation towards own problem conceptualization • Offer information/advice/solutions before active listening	• Purposeful, flexible application of communication skills • Ask clarifying questions to understand the problem in observable/measurable terms • Use a variety of communication skills (e.g., paraphrasing, summarizing, perception checking) in addition to asking questions • Active listening before offering information/advice/solutions • Communication skills used to build the consultation relationship

| About a Problem | • Student–deficit focus
• High inference problem definitions
• Constructed *for* consultee
• Jump prematurely into intervention stage
• Overwhelmed by so many problems | • Student–deficit focus or ecological focus
• Low inference (i.e., observable/measurable) or high inference problem definitions
• Constructed *for* consultee
• Jump prematurely into intervention stage
• Work quickly on several problems | • Ecological focus
• Low inference (i.e., observable/measurable) problem definitions
• Constructed *with* consultee
• Work systematically through problem-solving stages
• Work with consultee to prioritize problems |

Novice Consultation

Novice consultation is practiced by those such as graduate students prior to receiving consultation training or early in the training process, or practitioners with limited to no consultation training. Novice consultation may be reflected by a consultant's lack of awareness of particular communication skills or their purposes, or feeling robotic in their application (see Chapter 4). In novice consultation, a consultant may also be focused on being liked by the consultee (i.e., a personal relationship) rather than prioritizing the enhancement of the consultee's professional functioning (i.e., a professional working relationship), which we address in Chapter 3. There may not be a systematic problem-solving process, but a quick attempt to resolve a problem with advice.

Routine Consultation

Routine consultation refers to performing consultation without engaging in ongoing self-evaluation, goal-setting, and deliberate practice, the last of which refers to continuously practicing a skill while receiving ongoing corrective feedback (Rousmaniere, Goodyear, Miller, & Wampold, 2017). Veteran practitioners engaged in routine consultation may have a more nuanced understanding of school practice than novices (e.g., knowledge of systems and recognition of complexities in problem-solving), and may have engaged in more consultation over the years. However, time spent consulting without deliberate practice is unlikely to link with the development of competence or eventual expertise (Rousmaniere et al., 2017). Consequently, routine consultation tends to look more like what we define as novice consultation then what we define as competent consultation.

In routine consultation, a consultant may argue that there's not time to do formal, structured, or systematic consultation (or not be aware of or competent in the process), or that one cannot stop and think about what communication skills they should use at a given moment. In a routine context, consultation is viewed as asking questions, getting answers, and providing research-based solutions. In contrast, competent consultation includes a clear, systematic framework for practice including where, when, how often, and with whom consultation occurs, how communication ensues, and how problems are addressed.

Given gaps in the availability of supervision for school-based professionals (Chafouleas, Clonan, & Vanauken, 2002; Silva, Newman, Guiney, Valley-Gray, & Barrett, 2016), it is likely that many professionals are engaged in routine consultation. Further, routine consultation might be explained by a lack of extensive pre-service training in consultation or a lack of deep training in any particular consultation model; a school culture that is non-receptive to collaborative consultation often combined with a lack of skill in supporting or developing a culture in which consultation can occur; or an attempt to work as efficiently as possible, perhaps with limited training, in the time-crunched realities of schools (Newman, Hazel, Barrett, Das Chaudhuri, & Fetterman, 2017).

Whatever the explanation, *quick and dirty* or unsystematic modes of consultation are likely what many students observe in the field and engage in themselves during practicum and internship experiences. Or, they may not see supervisors or practitioners consulting at all. Tarquin and Truscott (2006) found practicum students and interns tend to observe supervisors engaged primarily in a special education assessment-driven role with a limited focus on consultation. In turn, trainees may go on to become early career practitioners engaging in unsystematic consultation practices with the justification of "this is what consultation looks like in the real world." Such practices become routine over time, creating a cyclic problem.

Competence in Consultation

The development of competence in professional psychology, and in school psychology as a specialty, has received increased attention over the past several years (e.g., Belar, 2009; Daly, Doll, Schulte, & Fenning, 2011; Fenning et al., 2015; Fouad et al., 2009). Competence is "an individual's capability and demonstrated ability to understand and do certain tasks in an appropriate and effective manner consistent with the expectations for a person qualified by education and training in a particular profession or specialty" (Kaslow, 2004, p. 775). Competence includes engaging in critical thinking and analysis, applying professional judgment in decision-making, and adapting decisions based on situational context (Newman, 2013).

Professional organizations have developed sets of competency in the domains of practice, including consultation. For example, the American Psychological Association (APA) Society of Consulting Psychology (Division 13) has specified 11 overarching competencies and 10 level-specific competencies for all consulting psychologists. The competencies are embedded in the overarching principles of adhering to a scientist-practitioner approach. The competencies are organized into personal, knowledge-based, and procedural domains with ethics and professionals standards providing a foundational anchor (see APA, 2017, for further details).

Several of these competencies (e.g., relationship development; diversity competence; assessment and intervention; process consultation) are particularly relevant for school consultants, as these competencies also link well to the National Association of School Psychologists' (NASP) *Standards for the Graduate Training and Preparation of School Psychologists* (2010b). The NASP consultation competencies are presented in Table 1.3. The importance of organizational competence is highlighted within and integrated across several APA Division 13 consultation competency areas. Organizational or systems-level understanding and intervention (Borgelt & Conoley, 1999; Curtis, Castillo, & Cohen, 2008; Newell & Coffee, 2015), including consulting on grade-, building-, and district-level teams, is also a pivotal competency area for school consultation. However, neither the NASP nor APA Division competencies provide sufficient specificity for the development of consultation skills.

TABLE 1.3 National Association of School Psychologists (NASP, 2010) Practice Model, Domain 2: Consultation and Collaboration

Summary	Examples of Professional Practices
School psychologists have knowledge of varied models and strategies of consultation, collaboration, and communication applicable to individuals, families, schools and systems, and methods to promote effective implementation of services. As part of a systematic and comprehensive process of effective decision-making and problem-solving that permeates all aspects of service delivery, school psychologists demonstrate skills to consult, collaborate, and communicate effectively with others.	1. Using a consultative problem-solving process for planning, implementing, and evaluating all instructional and mental and behavioral health services. 2. Facilitating effective communication and collaboration among families, teachers, community providers, and others. 3. Using consultation and collaboration when working at the individual, classroom, school, or systems levels. 4. Advocating for needed change at the individual student, classroom, building, district, state, or national levels.

A Developmental Approach to Consultation Competency Development

Although delineating competencies provides a helpful starting point to consider your development as a consultant, the framework is broad, leaving it challenging for the evaluation of growth (Newell, 2012). Furthermore, focusing too narrowly on competencies may result in "stove-piping," that is, mechanically listing competencies without recognizing how they are interrelated, interactive, and dynamic (Belar, 2009). Therefore, it may be helpful to view consultation competencies within a developmental framework, including matching appropriate training and supervision approaches with commensurate levels of CIT knowledge and skill levels (Rosenfield, 2012; Rosenfield et al., 2010; Stoltenberg, 1993).

As is illustrated in Figure 1.1, as you learn to consult it is theorized that you will move through the stages of developing awareness, conceptual understanding, skill acquisition, and skill application (Rosenfield et al., 2010). At the *awareness* level, you will have a cursory knowledge of theories, practices, and content, which develops into a deeper *conceptual understanding* of content, as well as more awareness of consultant-consultee relational dynamics. Eventually you will engage in *skill acquisition*, applying new skills in action for the first time in structured situations, followed by *application of skills* in context with increased automaticity and flexibility. To move along this continuum, particular training and supervision strategies may fit best at each level.

The particular methods of training proposed by Rosenfield et al. (2010) align with the "I do," "we do," "you do" didactic framework proposed by Archer and Hughes (2011) in their book *Explicit Instruction*. When a skill is brand new, "the best way to begin instruction is to show students what they are supposed to do,"

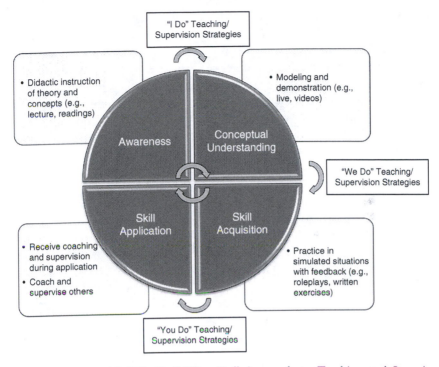

FIGURE 1.1 "I Do," "We Do," "You Do" Approach to Teaching and Learning Consultation.

including "demonstrating the skill and describing what is being done" (p. 29). Therefore, the "I do" stage, or modeling, should include clear, consistent, and concise modeling with several examples and your involvement with content. In this text, the "I do" stage includes our presentation of consultation content, videos of experts speaking about consultation, and examples of consultants in action, including a video model of contracting.

The "we do" stage, or prompted/guided practice, includes any of a number of scaffolds as you apply skills in action, including physical, verbal, or visual prompts. For example, as you are acquiring new skills you may practice consulting in a simulated problem-solving session while using a checklist as a visual prompt about what to do during that problem-solving stage. This text contains numerous activities, including simulated case examples, which can be supported by course instructors/supervisors to align with the "we do" stage. Much of this text is focused on the "we do" stage.

Finally, the "you do" stage, or unprompted practice, is when you perform a skill without any physical, verbal, or visual prompts. During this stage, performance monitoring and feedback continues to be essential. You can receive feedback through coaching or supervision, including audio- or video-recording and reviewing consultation sessions, transcribing, and engaging in written reflection all linked to action-oriented planning for the future (Newman, 2012). In Chapter 10 we highlight several actions for CITs as well as instructors and supervisors to use to support the increasingly independent application of school consultation in action.

One reason monitoring and feedback are critical even at later stages of skill development is because you may inadvertently be practicing errors (e.g., consistently asking questions in rapid sequence without listening actively or carefully to consultee responses). While *perfect* practice makes perfect, *imperfect* practice makes imperfect performance. For example, I (DN) recently began swimming daily with much enthusiasm and pleasure but limited skill. After a couple of months, my wife, a proficient swimmer, joined me at the pool and asked: "What the heck are you doing?" She provided verbal feedback on my breathing and strokes, as well as explicit modeling and physical prompts. It took continued deliberate practice, with her observation and feedback, to swim correctly and also to unlearn the poor habits I had practiced diligently. In other words, errors can be very difficult to undo once rehearsed a number of times (Archer & Hughes, 2011). The same is true of learning new consultation behaviors, and perhaps unlearning ineffective habits of practice.

Another aspect of training that we will focus upon is that of reflection. Doing is not enough—reflecting upon your actions facilitates learning. According to DiStefano, Gino, Pisano, and Staats (2014), learning is augmented "when individuals can not only 'do' but also 'think' about what they have been doing" (p. 4). They argue that "learning from direct experience can be more effective if coupled with reflection—that is, the intentional attempt to synthesize, abstract, and articulate the key lessons taught by experience" (p. 4). Their research shows that self-efficacy can be generated by reflection, as you make explicit your thinking about what you have learned. Their work confirms Schon's (1983) model of reflective practice as a critical adjunct to practitioner learning. Thus, we will provide some structures to enable you to reflect upon your experiences as a school consultant.

Finally, it is essential to recognize that learning to be a skilled consultant is not always easy or natural or comfortable. As in so many other areas, opportunities for learning often arise out of error and failure as much as success. Although focused on leadership training, Hackman and Wageman's (2007) wisdom resonates in our experience for CITs as well:

> failures generate data that can be mined for insight into how one's assumptions and models of action might be improved. Overcoming the impulse to reason defensively, however, can be a significant personal challenge. It … involves asking anxiety-arousing questions (e.g., about the validity of deeply held assumptions or about personal flaws in diagnosis or execution) … such activities are neither natural nor comfortable.
>
> *(p. 46)*

Hackman and Wageman go on to stress that emotional maturity is required "to move toward anxiety-arousing states of affairs in the interest of learning about them, rather than moving away from them to get anxieties reduced as quickly as possible" (p. 47).

The Need for Competent Consultants in Contemporary Schools

Undeniably, the educational landscape has changed a great deal over the past decade, potentially impacting how novice and experienced consultants enact consultation in contemporary school settings (Newman et al., 2017; Rosenfield, 2013). At least four educational issues seem to beg for increased attention to consultation training and practice: (1) the implementation of Multi-tiered Systems of Support (MTSS), or Response to Intervention (RtI); (2) increased national attention to issues of teacher training and practice; (3) burgeoning knowledge about the positive effects of collaboration; and (4) the increasing diversity of students.

MTSS/RtI

The implementation of the Individuals with Disabilities in Education Improvement Act (2004) brought with it the implementation of RtI in schools. RtI can be defined generally as "the practice of (1) providing high-quality instruction/intervention matched to student needs and (2) using learning rate over time and level of performance to (3) make important educational decisions" (Batsche et al., 2005, p. 5). According to Burns, Jimerson, VanDerHeyden, and Deno (2016), the term MTSS has become more common in educational vernacular, because unlike RtI, which developed from special education law, MTSS "focuses on providing instruction and intervention, rather than using data to identify disabilities" and "has a more explicit focus on general education" (Burns et al., 2016, p. 720). Therefore, we use the term MTSS throughout this text when discussing it in relation to school consultation, with RtI subsumed within MTSS. The precise convergence of school consultation and MTSS is not yet clear, although there seems to be some consensus that skilled consultation services are relevant, if not pivotal, to effective MTSS implementation (Gutkin & Curtis, 2009; Newman, Salmon, Cavanaugh, & Schneider, 2014; Reschly & Reschly, 2014). Team-based consultation services are usually integrated into MTSS processes, and much of the content of this text is useful for working with teams.

An essential component of MTSS is the concept of three tiers of service, each addressing concerns at a more intense level. We view consultation as relevant at *all tiers* of MTSS. For example, at Tier 1 (universal supports), school consultants might consult at a systems-level with administrators regarding school-wide academic or behavioral data, and observe and consult with teachers about either individual or class-wide issues. Notably, such consultations are prevention or well-being focused, with a goal of *giving psychology away* (Miller, 1969), working to improve systems and support large groups of students and staff. In some schools, consultation around individual students about whom teachers have questions is also in play. At Tier 2 (targeted intervention), school consultants are often active members of problem-solving teams and help select or design interventions and continue to be involved in data collection and analysis in collaboration with teachers and other consultees.

Consultation continues to be relevant at more intensive tiers, even at Tier 3 (intensive, individualized intervention), where a consultant can support a teacher consultee in working on an individual student concern. Sometimes, a concern can actually be indicative of problems at an earlier level (Tier 1 or 2), and the consultation provides an opportunity to affect more than the student who is initially of concern to the teacher. For example, a fourth-grade student with a severe problem in writing was one of several fourth-grade students referred to a school-based problem-solving team for writing concerns. Further examination revealed that the school did not have a consistent and explicit writing curriculum in the previous grades; as a result, students could not meet the expectations of the fourth-grade teachers. One of the outcomes was to move back to a Tier 1 intervention, the development of a school-wide writing program with specific competencies at each grade level. In sum, consultants must hold a flexible, prevention and systems-level orientation focusing on the nested systems in which problem-solving is situated rather than reifying Tiers as static entities or just another way to label students (e.g., "He's a Tier 3 kid.").

Consultation does not end at Tier 3. Even if a student qualifies for special education services, teachers supporting the student might need additional supports themselves. For example, general education teachers still might require consultative support regarding instruction in the general education setting, since students often still spend a good deal of instructional time in regular classrooms as part of their IEPs. Moreover, special education teachers can also benefit from consultation in their work with students (see, e.g., Tsakiris, 2012, and Pas, 2012, for how consultation can support special education teachers), such as conceptualizing differentiated instructional and intervention supports for students with a variety of needs.

Much of the content in this text around knowledge, skills, objectivity, and self-confidence applies to members of teams. For example, communication, relationships, and problem-solving are inherent in team-based services just as in dyadic consultation. An additional resource for teams is Teach Teamwork (www.apa.org/education/k12/teach-teamwork.aspx), a set of modules specifically addressed to building team processes, which may be freely accessed online (for additional information on team training, see Benishek et al., 2016; Rosenfield, Newell, Zwolski, & Benishek, 2018).

Teacher Professional Learning

A spotlight on teacher training, effectiveness, and evaluation burns brighter and hotter than ever before. In their book, *Professional Capital: Transforming Teaching in Every School*, Hargreaves and Fullan (2012) argue that "overload, isolation, increasing expectations, contradictory demands, and no real forum for ordinary teachers to make themselves heard" (p. 36) have been norms in teaching for decades and continue to persist and intensify in contemporary settings in spite of evidence that collaboration is increasingly viewed as a powerful mechanism for productive outcomes. Meanwhile, mounting evidence suggests teachers lack sufficient opportunities for professional development and professional collaboration at the in-service level (Darling-Hammond, Wei, Andree, Richardson, & Orphanos, 2009; Farbman, 2015). School consultation models focused on consultee empowerment may be viewed as forms of ongoing, embedded professional development for teachers and other educators.

The Value of Collaboration

Sarason (2003) concludes that: "If the conditions for productive learning do not exist for teachers, they cannot create and sustain those conditions for students" (p. 44). Consistent with this belief, evidence is emerging to suggest that collaborative approaches to professional learning result in positive outcomes for teachers (e.g., building strong working relationships) *and* students (e.g., enhancing academic achievement) (Darling-Hammond et al., 2009). Collaboration may be viewed as serving a social support function in schools, acting as a protective factor for teachers or others against stress, burnout, professional isolation, or professional stagnation (Conoley & Conoley, 2010; Hargreaves & Fullan, 2012). Collaboration can also be linked to the establishment of collective efficacy, namely, a group of educators' shared beliefs that they can make a difference for students, which has emerged as a significant factor influencing student achievement (Donohoo, 2017). Competent school consultants are in a position to collaborate effectively with teachers and to encourage collaboration in the school setting at large, ideally resulting in positive outcomes for teachers and students alike.

Student Diversity

An additional challenge is the growing diversity of students in schools in terms of culture, race, ethnicity, and language. The number of racial- and ethnic-minority students enrolled in public schools in the United States is larger than non-Hispanic White students and continues to increase (National Center for Education Statistics, 2016). However, the racial and ethnic diversity of educators lags significantly behind (Camera, 2015). Meeting the needs of students and staff in this increasingly complex world requires consultants to have an appreciation of cultural issues and skill in integrating this awareness into practice. In Chapter 2, we will further explore these variables.

The Need for Ethical Consultants in Contemporary Schools

Before moving on to discuss the framework of this book, there is an additional topic to be considered. The changing educational landscape and the organizational nature of work in school proliferate several ethical issues relevant to school consultation practice; yet ethics in school consultation is an area that has received less attention than would be expected. School-based practitioners, whether internal or external to a particular building or district, work at three different levels: with individuals, groups such as teams, and the school or district as an organization. Of course, some issues are relevant to all the activities of practitioners. Lowman and Cooper (2017) acknowledge the following concerns that are likely to raise ethical issues in practice with particular relevance to consultants: (a) competence, (b) contracting and informed consent, (c) confidentiality, (d) multiple relationships, (e) conflicts of interest, (f) failure to use research science and evidence-based practices, and (g) conflicts between organizational demands and ethics.

Competence

Working within your competency areas is an ethical expectation, which is why becoming a competent school consultant is an ethical issue. Developing multicultural competence for working with diverse student, parent, and school staff is also a generic ethical issue that has a significant relationship to consultation. The NASP *Ethical and Professional Practices for School Psychologists Guidelines* (2010a) Standard 2.01, in discussing competence, also includes understanding "factors associated with age, gender, gender identity, race, ethnicity, culture, national origin, religion, sexual orientation, disability, language or socioeconomic status" in providing services. This issue will be further discussed in Chapter 2.

Contracting, Informed Consent, and Confidentiality

Lowman and Cooper (2017) have found that even the most recent edition of the APA Code of Ethics does not pay sufficient attention to the practice of psychology in organizations, although the 2002 revision did include Standard 3.11, Psychological Services Delivered to or Through Organizations. This standard addresses contracting and the informed consent process; in Chapter 6, some of these specific ethical issues will be elaborated upon, along with the limits of privacy and confidentiality.

Multiple Relationships and Conflicts of Interest

Ethics codes also discuss concerns related to multiple relationships. In the complex culture of schools, multiple relationships are common. For example, teachers and other staff develop personal friendships, which sometimes become a concern when they impair the objectivity or the effectiveness of professionals in conducting their professional functions, including consultation. In one case, the teacher backed out of the process for personal reasons; because the CIT and the teacher had developed a personal relationship, the CIT was so sympathetic to the teacher that she did not suggest some alternatives that might have allowed the consultation to continue, depriving the student client of further intervention support. In many situations, multiple individuals are involved, and their needs and interest can be in conflict. For example, a bilingual teacher scheduled a group of students at a convenient time for the bilingual teacher's schedule, but the students were not well matched for their needs. A CIT working with the classroom teacher and the bilingual teacher saw that the student they were concerned about was not making progress and losing class time as well, but found it difficult to address the conflict of interest between the bilingual teacher's scheduling issues and the teacher's concern about the student's progress.

Failure to Use Research Science and Evidence-Based Practices

While there are not always evidence-based practices and research to support all assessment and intervention activities, there is a priority for consultants to include them in their work. However, consultants work indirectly, and the consultee is usually responsible for the implementation. These issues are addressed in multiple chapters of this book, especially Chapter 8.

Conflicts Between Organizational Demands and Ethics

All school practitioners are sometimes faced with this type of issue, but it can be especially difficult for consultants. Most consultants lack power within the organization, although their consultation and advocacy skills are the tools they have to try to work through these issues when they arise. Consultants often see processes in schools that are mandated but not in the best interests of some of the students and staff with whom they work. There are no easy answers to these kinds of questions. For example, grade retention is often a recognized intervention in a school by administrators at the school and district level, but not an empirically supported strategy. When it is recommended by the teacher but perceived as not in the best interest of a particular child about whom the teacher has requested consultation, it is difficult to challenge.

A Framework for School Consultation

The School Consultation (SC) framework presented in this text reflects our own assumptions and beliefs about consultation, which are built upon both scientific evidence and practice experience. Several consultation models are reflected in SC, including Consultee-Centered Consultation (Caplan, 1970; Lambert, Hylander, & Sandoval, 2004; Newman & Ingraham, 2017; Sandoval, 2014); Instructional Consultation (Rosenfield, 1987; Rosenfield, Gravois, & Silva, 2014); Process Consultation (Schein, 1999, 2009, 2013, 2016); Multicultural School Consultation (Ingraham, 2000, 2014); Behavioral/Problem-Solving Consultation

(Bergan & Kratochwill, 1990; Kratochwill, Altschaefl, & Bice-Urbach, 2014); and Organizational Consultation (Illback, 2014).

In Chapter 2, we introduce the concept of school culture and the process of entry into the school as a consultant. We examine the rationale for assessing the culture of a school in which you plan to provide services as a consultant, beginning with a historical overview of staff collaboration in American schools; introduce the concepts of norms and regularities in organizational life, and provide some activities to support your understanding; examine some multicultural parameters related to consultation; and provide strategies for assessing school culture and for increasing your opportunity for effective entry into the school.

In Chapter 3, relationships are the focus. We describe the differences between working relationships and personal relationships; discuss the expert-collaborative continuum in consultation; examine the perils of being the helper versus the helpee; the importance of self-knowledge as a consultant; and how to conduct difficult conversations that arise in your relationships.

In Chapter 4, the communication skills that will support and enhance your work are presented. We agree with Kegan and Lahey (2001) "that work settings are language communities" (p. 8), and your awareness of, and skill in, how you communicate with your consultee is essential to becoming a competent consultant. The impact of language on creating the problem to be addressed will be described and nuances that distinguish between communication skills in consultation and counseling considered. The specific strategies include: (a) listening and the challenges that listening involves; (b) obtaining information through clarification and questioning; (c) paraphrasing to ensure that the consultee's communication is clear; and (d) perception checking to acknowledge that feelings and emotions are also heard. Activities to practice your skills are included in the chapter as well.

Chapter 5 provides a brief history of how problem-solving emerged from research into clinical work. The stages of problem-solving that will be elaborated on in the following chapters are introduced here.

It is critical that the purpose and processes of consultation are transparent to the consultee, especially if the consultation model is collaborative. Obtaining informed consent of the consultee to engage in the process is key. In Chapter 6, the rationale for *Contracting* is explored, along with providing the nuts and bolts of the contracting process. Activities to practice contracting are provided.

It is not intervention but *Problem Identification and Analysis (PID/PA)* that is the critical first step in problem-solving—any intervention must address the right problem. Chapter 7 introduces the four different types of consultee problems that you will encounter (lack of knowledge, skill, objectivity, and confidence) and provides the nuts and bolts of the *PID/PA* process. The chapter also presents six Big Ideas that undergird the *PID/PA* process, along with activities to support building your problem identification and analysis skills.

Designing and implementing intervention skills are the focus of Chapter 8, which covers two related stages: (1) *Intervention Planning* and (2) *Intervention*

Implementation, Monitoring, and Performance Feedback. Once again, the details of the process are explored. The importance of the consultant supporting the implementation and documenting that the intervention has actually taken place are critical aspects of these stages.

Consultation is a relationship, so it is important to say hello (contracting) and goodbye (closure), whether or not the problem has been resolved. Chapter 9 addresses the nuts and bolts of *Post-Intervention Planning and Closure (PIPC)*. Sometimes the closure stage leads to a new issue for consultation, or it simply leaves the door open for a future opportunity.

The final chapter, Chapter 10, introduces the concept that this is just the beginning of your consultation training and experience. In Chapter 10, we provide a roadmap for continuing learning to be a consultant. Assessing your consultation skills and the outcomes of your consultation work are ongoing processes requiring feedback, supervision, and deliberate practice. We hope that the final chapter will encourage you to expand your thinking about consultation training and how to move toward becoming an ever more competent consultation professional.

Making the Most of This Text

You will benefit most from this text if you are taking a course in consultation and are placed in a school site to engage in studying the culture and conducting entry as a consultant, as well as engaging in problem-solving consultation activities as you work your way through the book. Involvement in the school, whether with students or adults, can be an anxiety-producing activity, but a necessary one in order to develop your skills—consider reframing your anxiety to excitement as you begin the path to competence. Becoming a competent school consultant is not just about learning academics/knowledge but about working as a novice professional in a school building under quality supervision, and that includes developing competence in consultation as well. See Video 1.1, an introduction to this book, by one of the authors, Dr. Sylvia Rosenfield.

If you do not have the advantage of classmates to discuss your responses to activities and skill development strategies, you might consider asking a colleague or fellow student to join you; or, you might participate in a study group in your professional setting. It is important in any case that you be comfortable with how much you want to share about your responses as well as to be respectful in how you respond to your partner(s) as you work your way through this text, using the opportunity to build trust and open communication.

As you read the book, you will find a number of recurring features in each chapter. Each chapter begins with a quick write reflection activity, to help you identify your thinking and assumptions about the topic of the chapter. Within the chapters, there will be opportunities for you to engage in individual and group activities, and the text will alert you and your class instructor, if you are in a consultation course, to activities that we have found useful in the class context. We also offer a number of models of how consultants might strategically use language during consultation. We hope these examples serve as building blocks to aid you in finding your own consultation voice. Finally, experts on school consultation and problem-solving discuss, and sometimes model, aspects of the consultation process in videos linked to pertinent content throughout the book. We hope these videos act as resources to further support your understanding of school consultation, provided by voices in addition to our own.

Back to Assumptions and Goals About School Consultation

How does school consultation as we have defined and contextualized it here fit with what you previously thought? Based on our collective experiences educating CITs, we imagine that many of you are thinking school consultation is more complex than what you expected. Indeed, complicating your thinking about consultation is an outcome of learning to consult (Worrell, Naecker, Gerchow, Green, Kunesh, & Casey, 2017). In the chapters that follow, we further explore key facets of school consultation overviewed in this introduction and pair this content with interactive training activities. As you work through the text, we encourage you to continue to question your assumptions about consultation and to set goals for your knowledge and skill development. Activities throughout this text will help you do just that for this initial stage of learning.

ACTIVITY 1.2 (INDIVIDUAL)

Developing Your Own Map of Consultation

At the beginning of this chapter, you wrote down your initial thoughts about consultation. Now take your initial sentences/thoughts and your new knowledge from this chapter and design a map to diagram your current understanding of school consultation. Underneath the map, write a brief written summary of your map. We will revisit this map at the end of the book to see how your understanding of school consultation evolves over time.

2

UNDERSTANDING SCHOOL CULTURE

What is essential is invisible to the eye.
(Antoine de Saint-Exupery, The Little Prince)

Consultation does not take place in a vacuum. Every school has a culture that serves as an important context for consultation services. When we make the commitment to help the residents in that culture to make change, it is essential that we bring understanding of that culture into our awareness and our actual work. The culture view is critical, since as participants in the culture, we too often fail to see that it is the culture, rather than the individual, that has an impact on the behavior of those within the culture: because we cannot "*see the structure in the same way that one sees an individual … we have trouble grasping and acting in terms of its existence*" (italics in the original; Sarason, 1982, p. 27). In this chapter, we will focus on helping you to develop that awareness as well as learn the importance of the entry process into that culture. Learning how to enter a school with consultation as an important aspect of your service delivery is a critical skill.

To begin, consider these warm-up questions regarding school culture.

ACTIVITY 2.1 (INDIVIDUAL)

Warm-Up Questions: School Culture

Write down your own responses to the following questions. You can write sentences or just key words.

1. What is your definition of culture?
2. How do you define collaboration? What do you see as the benefits of collaboration?

3. How would you go about entering into a new school setting with the goal of providing services as a consultant?
4. How do the assumptions teachers, administrators, and other professionals in the school have about the school consultant role at your practicum or internship site impact the entry process? What are the implications for engaging in consultation?

What Do We Mean by Culture?

Much of the professional psychology literature on culture focuses on multicultural and cross-cultural issues, often on the race, gender, or ethnicity of those involved in treating and treatment. Too often, culture is viewed as a variable or category of variable, not as "a paradigm or worldview that permeates one's thoughts and actions" (Ingraham, 2014, p. 343). As one consultant in training (CIT) stated:

> Initially, I had great difficulties understanding school culture probably because I did not relate the concept of culture to school. My understanding of culture has always related to ethnicity and race. Thus, culture as an environmental component was difficult for me to grasp. The environmental component of culture seemed so abstract.

Perhaps no one has better articulated the concept of school culture and its profound effect on the work of those in schools than Sarason, especially in his classic book, *The Culture of the School and the Problem of Change* (1971, 1982). Much of our work as school consultants involves change, and sometimes these changes conflict with cultural regularities of those with whom we work. For example, a programmatic regularity in many schools, as we will detail below, is a belief in teachers working independently, even though current research supports teacher collaboration (e.g., Donohoo, 2017). Lowman (2015) reminds us "consultants are always crossing cultural boundaries, even within their own cultures, because every organization they work with has a unique culture of its own, as do the groups and individuals within those organizations" (p. x).

Organizational Culture of Schools

So, what do we need to know as consultants about the culture of schools? First, schools are organizational settings with unique cultures. Secondly, collaboration and consultation have not always been the way the work is done. While collaborative structures have become more commonplace in American schools, serving multiple functions, such structures are relatively new (e.g., Hargreaves & Fullan, 2012; Huberman, 1993; Lortie, 1975). Huberman (1993) characterized teachers historically as "independent artisans" working within the privacy of their own class-room while having periodic contact with colleagues to expand their knowledge and skills. More recently, Hord (2008) found that there has been a profound "shift in the glacier of isolation" (p. 10), with fewer barriers to teacher interaction so that teachers now come together to share their work. It has taken over 100 years for seri-ous opposition to an individualistic model of schooling to develop (Lortie, 1975).

But these roots in independence and isolation continue to impact school cul-ture, even as school staff members have sought to move to more collaborative structures. The current accountability focus is on an individual teacher's student test scores, so it is not surprising that teachers may still see themselves as isolated within the context of their own classroom. In fact, across systems and organiza-tions in the United States, a primary goal is to optimize and reward individual performance, as true in the schools as in our society at large (Quintero, 2017). Although we may pay lip service to collaboration and teamwork, developing the skills to maximize the benefits of collaboration remains a work in progress (Rosenfield, Newell, Zwolski, & Benishek, 2018).

What has generated the push for collaboration and teaming in schools? Research and policy have identified collaboration and teaming as structures enabling schools to more effectively educate an increasingly diverse population of students. Student diversity, including culture, race, ethnicity, and language, has generated concern about how best to address all students' educational and mental health needs. Along with the increased diversity of the student population, and in part, a response to that diversity, there has been a proliferation of specialists, such as reading teach-ers; teachers who support students whose first language is not English; and men-tal health providers, such as school counselors and school psychologists, leading to the fragmentation of services. Thus, this development has accelerated the need for collaborative structures, including co-teaching, consultation, and teams. It has also increased the need for comprehensive professional service delivery approaches requiring collaboration at the district, school, and classroom levels (Gravois, 2013). Even as schools have developed overarching policies such as Multi-tiered Systems of Support (MTSS), consultation and collaboration within those systems remain important skills for effective implementation of services to students.

Furthermore, policy options such as mainstreaming and least restrictive envi-ronment in special education law have increased the amount of time that students experiencing academic and behavioral issues spend in regular education settings rather than isolated in special education settings. These policies have enhanced the need for collaboration among regular educators and specialists, a collaboration that is still being negotiated (Pugach, Blanton, & Correa, 2011). Because of the concerns around the special education process and the least restrictive environ-ment policies, researchers and practitioners have turned to teams with different names and structures, generically termed problem-solving teams. These teams are intended to reduce the number of inappropriate referrals for special education evaluation and provide support to teachers who were increasingly being assigned difficult to teach and manage students. Although these teams do not have a strong research base (Rosenfield et al., 2018), they have proliferated in the schools since their emergence in the 1970s and 1980s (Truscott, Cohen, Sams, Sanborn, & Frank, 2005).

As the problem-solving team structures were developing, schools were also incorporating more collaborative structures in other areas, including teacher professional development and school reform (Hord, 2008). A growing literature emerged about teachers' workplace, detailing how school culture affected teachers' knowledge, skills, and morale. For example, Little (2007) describes how a professional community can empower "teachers' effectiveness and strengthen the overall capacity of a school to pursue improvements" and how "a collective responsibility for student success" (p. 54) has become associated with student achievement. Yet she recognized the continuing tensions that undercut collaboration in schools, including "the difficult balance between collaborative endeavors and individual interests, and the sheer demand that collaboration places on time and energy" (p. 54), particularly in schools that do not value collaboration. This is especially problematic given current accountability measures that focus on the academic performance of an individual teacher's students.

The school reform movement also embraced collaboration and teaming, with the need for staff to collaborate on decisions and implementation of change (e.g., Hord, 2008). The concept of a school that learns involved team learning as key to improvement, with collaboration to "be fostered inside classrooms, between parents and teachers, among members of the community, and in the 'pilot groups' that pursue successful school change" (Senge et al., 2000, pp. 7–8). Just as in other organizational settings, Senge's work spoke to educators as a way to foster improvement and change.

However, insufficient attention has been paid to training and implementation issues as educators seek to change and sustain a more collaborative school culture. While the power of collaboration has been acknowledged, several authors have reflected on the difficulty of moving to an effective culture of collaboration (e.g., Hargreaves & Fullan, 2012). Early on, Kruse, Louis, and Bryk (1994) concluded that structural elements (e.g., time) in reform proposals were receiving more attention than social and human resources (e.g., interpersonal relationships). A number of authors have raised the larger issue of whether schools as organizations are conducive to teams and collaboration (e.g., Doll et al., 2005; Pugach et al., 2011). One of the purposes of this book is to alert you, as a new consultant, to the culture issues that have the capacity to impede or enhance your collaboration with other school staff as you seek to embed consultation services into your work.

Organizational Boundaries

Schools have permeable boundaries with the community. In this text, we have not focused on family or community, both of which groups are relevant to the work of school consultants. Our focus has been on the school. However, family caregivers are also key participants in the workings of the school. The Conjoint Behavioral Consultation (CBC) model, now referred to as Teachers and Parents as Partners (TAPP), is a unique consultation approach in that it includes caregivers as part of the behavioral consultation problem-solving process (Sheridan & Kratochwill, 2008). By including caregivers, family-school partnerships can be strengthened in support of students (Sheridan, Clarke, & Christensen, 2014). A full review of CBC/TAPP is beyond the scope of this book, but research (including randomized control studies) by Sheridan and colleagues on CBC/TAPP has consistently demonstrated enhanced academic, social–emotional, and behavioral outcomes for students (see Sheridan, Clarke, & Ransom, 2014, and the Teachers and Parents as Partners website for comprehensive summaries).

Learning About Norms and Regularities That Impact Helping

Sarason acknowledged that the "helping role inevitably involves changing someone or something," and that people, not just school staff, "do not take kindly to departures from their accustomed ways of thinking and acting even when they proclaim they are motivated to do so" (Sarason, 1995, p. 66). In order to help that change, he believed it was critical to learn about "how their structure, practices, regularities, goals, and rationales combine as justification for what is and rejection of alternatives about what could or should be" (Sarason, 1995, p. 66). The culture view is critical, since as participants in the culture, we too often fail to see that it is the culture, rather than the individual, that has an impact on the behavior of those within the culture.

ACTIVITY 2.2 (INDIVIDUAL, GROUP)

Man From Mars

Read the following excerpt from Sarason (1996), and answer the subsequent questions individually. If possible, compare responses with a partner or in a small group.

Let us approach the general problem of outcomes by indulging in a fantasy. Imagine a being from outer space who finds himself and his invisible space platform directly above an elementary school. Being superior to earthly beings, he is able to see everything that goes on in the school. But he does operate under certain restrictions: he does not comprehend the meaning of written or spoken language, and it can never occur to him that things go on inside of what we call heads. He can see and hear everything and, being an *avant-garde* outer-spacer, he, of course, possesses a kind of computer that records and categorizes events on any number of dimensions, allowing him to discern what we shall call the existing regularities. (Let me anticipate the discussion of the latter part of this chapter by advancing the hypothesis that *any attempt to introduce change into the school setting requires, among other things, changing the existing regularities in some way.*

The intended outcomes involve changing an existing regularity, eliminating one or more of them, or producing new ones.)

Let us start with one of the more obvious regularities. Our outer-spacer will discern (but not understand) that for five consecutive days, the school is densely populated, while for two consecutive days, it is devoid of humans. That puzzles him. Why this 5-2 pattern? Why not a 4-3 or some other kind of pattern like 2-1-2-1-1?

What if the outer-spacer could talk to us and demanded an explanation for this existing regularity? Many of us earthlings would quickly become aware that we have a tendency to assume that the way things are is the way things should be. But our outer-spacer persists. Is this the way it has always been? Is this the way it is in other countries? Is it demonstrably the best pattern for achieving the purposes of schooling? Does the existing regularity reflect noneducational considerations like religion, work patterns, and leisure time? Is it possible that the existing regularity has no intrinsic relationship to learning and education?

From Sarason, S.B. (1996). *Revisiting "The culture of school and the problem of change."* (p. 96). New York: Teachers College Press.

Questions for Reflection:

1. According to this passage, how do you define an existing regularity?
2. Name a few school-based regularities that you are aware of/have noticed from your own experiences as a student or working in the schools?
3. Why do you think each of these regularities was in place?
4. What are some alternatives to the existing regularities you identified?

Maital (2017) makes the case even more complex, as she reminds us that our consultees, as well as consultants, often have hidden competing commitments and competing priorities. Citing the work of Kegan and Leahy (2001) on competing commitments, Maital finds that even after developing skills in consultation, energy may continue to be devoted to goals or beliefs counter to using those skills: "psychologists, trained to seek intrapsychic factors in individual difficulties, may assume that reliance on … consultation may not really resolve psychological difficulties" (p. 246). It is not unusual in our experience for consultants to express the concern that they might miss the real problem if they consult with the teacher rather than do a complete traditional psychoeducational assessment. When we take an ecological perspective on problems brought to us within any school, we are, in part, moving away from a deficit approach to concerns and acknowledging that it is the roles and relationships within a school that define how goals and problems will be approached. In many cases, this will present a conflict with the norms and regularities that structure the way the school culture has viewed problem behavior in students.

To develop a clearer sense of the concept of norms, you might begin by examining those within your own university class or professional development unit.

ACTIVITY 2.3 (INDIVIDUAL, GROUP)

Assessing Norms and Regularities in Your Class Culture

Individually, complete the survey below. Next answer the subsequent questions individually and, if possible, compare responses with your classmates.

In any class there are informal "dos" and "don'ts." They are rarely written down, but they serve as a kind of code, making it clear what people in the system should and should not do if they are to be accepted by others. Below is a list of specific things that a student or instructor might do or say. Estimate what most people in your consultation class would feel about each item (not what you feel, but what you think others would feel). That is, **what do you feel the predominant feeling of most of the students in this class** is concerning whether one should or should not do or say the thing in question? You can indicate your answer by placing a check mark in the appropriate column beside each item.

The majority of students feel that someone	Should	Should Not
1. Ask others who seem upset to express their feelings directly		
2. Tell colleagues what you really think of their work		
3. Look for ulterior motives in other students' behavior		
4. Avoid disagreement and conflict whenever possible		
5. Question ways of doing things		
6. Disagree with the instructor if you happen to know more about the issue than s/he does		
7. Withhold personal feelings and stick to the merits of the case		
8. Push for new ideas even if they are vague or unusual		
9. Ask others to tell you what they really think of your work		
10. Keep your real thoughts and reactions to yourself, by and large		
11. Trust others not to take advantage of you		
12. Be skeptical about things		
13. Point out other people's mistakes, to improve working effectiveness		
14. Listen to others' ideas, but reserve the decision to yourself		
15. Try out new ways of doing things even if it is uncertain how they will work out		
16. Stay cool—keep your distance from others		

Questions for Reflection:

1. What are the items you think the majority of students would feel some-one "Should" do? What are the implications?
2. What are the items you think the majority of students would feel some-one "Should Not" do? What are the implications?
3. If you do this with your class, what are the items in which the class split? What are the implications?
4. Would you like to see some changes in the norms? Why? What would be the implications of those changes?

Sarason (1996) reminds us that the existing culture is one of many possible alternatives, even though that may not be obvious to those living within the current culture. To focus attention on this perspective, Sarason created a "man from Mars" who lands on earth and seeks to understand why things are done the way they are in schools. By doing this, he helps us to see the arbitrariness of some of our norms—like why schools operate from September to June in most places and are empty during the summer months. Is that really the only calendar for schools to operate on? Generating an alternative is tough because it requires us to change our actions, our thinking, and how the setting will operate. When some schools in the United States tried to move to an all-year schedule, with breaks scattered throughout the year, it was difficult for many communities to adjust to that model. Or, more recently in some school districts, arguments have been made in favor of changing school start times to allow high school students a later start than elementary students, given myriad, positive effects that have been demonstrated from such a change that takes into account adolescent sleep patterns. This effort has encountered opposition, in part because it is different from how things have been done before. The newscast in Video 2.1 discusses this some more.

Recognizing how difficult it is to change a norm or regularity in schools, Sarason (1996) asks us to acknowledge "there are no better ways to comprehend the culture of the school than either by looking at how it responds to pressures for change or how it responds to someone who is trying to be helpful to people within it" (p. vii). A good place to begin to understand how change will be perceived in a school in which you are working is by answering questions about the norms, regularities, and unwritten rules about help-seeking and working with a consultant.

ACTIVITY 2.4 (INDIVIDUAL, GROUP)

Norms and Regularities, Outcomes, and Alternative Regularities

1. Individually, or as a class, read through the example.
2. Individually complete the first alternative regularities for the regularity, "teachers do not ask for help."
3. Individually think of additional norms/regularities, intended outcomes, and alternatives for the final row. Although there is only one blank row, it might be helpful to think of more than one series of norms, outcomes, and alternatives.
4. In a small group or individually, discuss/reflect on your responses guided by these questions:

   a. Do the intended outcomes and actual outcomes of the norms you investigated converge or diverge?

   b. If the intended outcomes diverge from the actual outcomes, what are some alternative possibilities to achieve the intended outcomes?

   c. How do you think a school consultant might support the consideration of alternative regularities in a school when intended outcomes are divergent from actual outcomes?

Norms/Regularities/ Unwritten Rules in Your School	Intended Outcomes (What are the regularities supposed to accomplish?)	Actual Outcomes (What do the regularities actually accomplish?)	Alternative Regularities (What are some different ways to do things?)
School psychologists primarily function as "testers" and special education gatekeepers	• Get at root of problem • Put a label on it for parents • Provide "comprehensive" recommendations • Meet school's legal obligations • Get kids in special education, which is more effective • "Professional preciousness" • Fits with professional training • Shifting roles would be hard	• Focus on student, miss alternative roles for school psychologist • Ecological perspectives in problem-solving • Cross-disciplinary collaboration • Clear assessment questions • Recommendations linked to instruction	• Alternative roles for school psychologist • Ecological perspectives in problem-solving • Cross-disciplinary collaboration • Clear assessment questions • Recommendations linked to instruction

Teachers do not ask for help	• Avoid negative evaluation, criticism/save face • Avoid lengthy processes that may be ineffective • Maintain professional autonomy	• Professional isolation • Students may not get what they need • Focus on student (fundamental attribution error)	?
?	?	?	?

Assumptions That Impact Consultation

Embedded in this activity around norms is a set of assumptions that impact school consultation work. Here are some very important assumptions that are critical to the success of the school consultant.

Broken Child Versus Mismatch

In a school, is the problem referred to the consultant or the problem-solving team viewed as situated (a) within the child, or (b) within the relationship between the student's skills, the teacher's skills, and other issues within the context? If there is a substantial difference between the school culture, the individual consultee, and the consultant, awareness of that discrepancy is essential. In one situation (Pickering, 2012), the school culture and teacher consultee valued retention of students not reaching standards in kindergarten, while the consultant-in-training (CIT) was focused on research that recommended promotion and was focused on an intervention to support the student building his early reading skills. The teacher was less focused on the student making progress, as she had already decided he should be retained in kindergarten for another year. In another example, the school psychologist was so wedded to the broken child assumption that he could not refrain from assessing the student's cognitive and achievement profile when he was developing his consultation skills, in case he "missed a learning disability."

Value of Collaboration and Consultation

We have earlier provided you an introduction to the history of collaboration in schools. Within each school, collaboration can be valued along a continuum, and it is important that you assess the school, your consultee, and yourself. Sometimes school psychologists so value their role as experts that they are less willing to develop collaborative relationships with teachers. We have heard school psychologists state that they are unwilling to give up their expert role. Of course, psychologists maintain their expertise as psychologists and as experts in the process of consultation, confusing their role in assessment with their expertise in general. In some schools, the culture is one of self-reliance, and teachers are expected to resolve their own problems or send any student exhibiting problems for special education assessment. Such schools have been described as balkanized cultures (Hargreaves & Fullan, 2012).

Hargreaves and Fullan (2012) describe collaboration at the school level along a continuum. There can be *comfortable collaboration*, where teachers get along but do not work on problems together. This can be puzzling to a novice consultant. In one school, teachers ate together and planned parties together but did not work together on school, classroom, or curriculum concerns. While it seemed collegial, the collaboration was not about the work. Sometimes an administrator can attempt to encourage collaboration, setting up time to meet and organizing teams for different purposes. This *contrived collegiality* can be seen in schools where time is allocated for meetings, but teachers are observed grading papers and on their smartphones rather than focusing on working together. Of course, some teams may function better than others, but it is important to be aware of the lack of a culture of collaboration among a group with which you as a consultant want to work. A more promising setting for consultation is schools that have an interactive and functional professional culture, in which consultation and collaboration thrive. While most schools have a mixture of these types of collaboration, the consultant needs to be alert to the impact on consultation of these varying levels of collaboration.

Multicultural Issues in School Consultation

Although it is critical that school consultants have the requisite consultation skills, application of those skills in culturally diverse settings requires additional training. Ingraham's (2000) Multicultural School Consultation (MSC) framework consists of five components designed to bring a multicultural lens to the practice of consultation. MSC integrates cultural sensitivity and awareness into the consultation process at all levels, from entry to intervention implementation.

- The first component, Consultant Learning and Development, summarizes knowledge and skill areas expected of culturally competent consultants, including understanding one's own culture, others' cultures, and the impact of culture in supporting consultees and clients.
- Consultee Learning and Development, the second component, focuses on the knowledge, skill, objectivity, and confidence areas for consultees that might be supported during the consultation process.
- Component 3, Cultural Variations in the Consultation Constellation (Figure 2.1), highlights cultural similarities and differences between consultants,

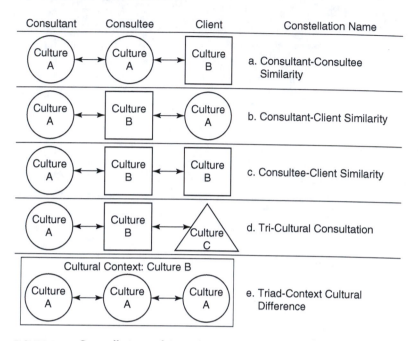

FIGURE 2.1   Constellations of Consultation Relationships (Ingraham, 2000).

consultees, and clients, and how these might be relevant to the consultation process.

- The fourth component is Contextual and Power Influences, which explores power differentials between individuals engaging in the consultation and also considers the nested systems in which the consultation takes place.

- The final component is Hypothesized Methods for Supporting Consultee and Client Success, which includes the consultant's careful construction of a problem frame in collaboration with the consultee, incorporating culturally responsive consultation strategies and continuing, always, to engage in professional learning and self-reflection about culture.

The complexity of multicultural consultation goes beyond the knowledge base. Miranda (2016) provides a series of cases that support a more culturally sensitive school consultation practice. We will come back to these issues in later chapters. As both Miranda (this chapter), and Ingraham (Chapter 4) describe in their videos, the development of multicultural and cross-cultural school consultation competency development is an ongoing process for all of us. Once you have developed increased self-awareness around these issues, you can seek out additional resources and consult with more knowledgeable others (e.g., supervisors) regarding your areas of need; developing a plan for further learning can include applied experiences during your professional training.

Dr. Antoinette Miranda presents here some interesting aspects of the urban multicultural context in Video 2.2.

In a consultation case, it is important to examine the cultural constellation to determine relevance of cultural issues to the process, consistent with the third component of Ingraham's (2000) Multicultural School Consultation framework (Figure 2.1). Pickering (2012) provides a good example of a cultural consultation constellation issue in a case in which the CIT identified with the student who shared his ethnic background. In another case, one CIT was concerned about a dysfunctional grade-level team with which she was working on a curriculum assessment issue. Three of the teachers were white and one was African-American; the three white teachers had bonded into a group, and the African-American teacher was not participating in the team meetings. The CIT had not considered this as part of the constellation until it was pointed out in supervision.

ACTIVITY 2.5 (INDIVIDUAL, GROUP)

Cultural Constellation

If you are currently consulting with a consultee or consultees, complete and answer the following questions. Answer the subsequent questions.

1. Identify the constellation of your consultation triad in the Figure 2.1.
2. What are the implications of this constellation for your work, if any?
3. How do you determine if cultural issues are *salient* in your case?
4. Discuss your responses with a partner.

Globalization of School Psychology Consultation

Before leaving the topic of multicultural consultation, it is relevant to introduce the growth of a global perspective in psychology. There is increasing interest in globalization across school psychology as well as a history of school psychologists with an interest in consultation theory, training, practice, and research connecting with one another around the world (see, for example, Hatzichristou & Rosenfield, 2017). Psychologists from Australia, Canada, England, Greece, Hong Kong, Israel, Sweden, and the United States contributed chapters to the

International Handbook of Consultation in Educational Settings (Hatzichristou & Rosenfield, 2017), which provides a resource to learn more about this aspect of school consultation.

Strategies for Uncovering School Culture

We are hopeful that you are now considering how important it is to focus on school culture rather than just on the problems of individual children. Rhona Weinstein, a clinical psychology faculty member at the UC-Berkeley, attending a Carnegie Conference on Urban Schools, commented most eloquently on looking in at schools:

> I think we need to teach psychologists about schooling—getting to know classrooms and schools and the children, teachers, and principals inside of schools. Those of us with interest in schooling share a fascination with the personality of classroom and schools and districts, much like others' fascination with the personality of individuals. We need to instill this excitement and raise awareness of the importance of schooling environments in children's development.

Where are some places you can learn about a school culture? For sure, one place is the school faculty meeting. To prepare for such a visit, here is an activity you can do by yourself or with your consultation class:

ACTIVITY 2.6 (INDIVIDUAL, GROUP)

School Culture Case Example

Read the following case example and then answer the subsequent questions individually and, if possible, compare responses with a partner or in a small group.

Case Example:

You are asked at a faculty meeting to introduce yourself as the new school psychologist and to talk about consultation. The principal introduces you to the staff and announces that the superintendent has indicated interest in the school's participation in building more collaborative working relationships among staff, including the school psychologist. However, he states that the program is voluntary.

The principal runs into your time by making several announcements regarding school procedures. As you finally get up to talk, some teachers listen attentively while others chat with each other. When you ask for questions, there is a pause. Then one teacher asks how this collaboration thing differs from other new programs that have come and gone in the past. Others ask what proof there is that consultation makes a difference for students and how much extra work is involved for teachers.

Questions for Reflection:

1. What information did you pick up from the meeting about the norms and regularities of this school culture?
2. What information did you pick up about the roles of the principal and the teachers?
3. What else is it important for you to confirm/learn about this school culture?
4. Taking an ecological point of view, how might you have responded to these questions?

Other ways you can learn about school culture include:

- Talking with individual teachers about their experiences with consulting and collaborating with colleagues,
- Spending time in the teacher lounge and listening to conversations,
- Sitting in on team meetings at the grade and school level,
- Interviewing the principal about consultation and collaboration as a school norm.

Additional information can be gleaned from parents, of course, and from students, who may have little or no opportunity to collaborate with each other. In fact, students are often the most perceptive purveyors of the school culture. One high school student mentioned that she knew how the teachers felt about her school because they couldn't get out of the building fast enough when the afternoon bell rang.

Developing a map of the relationships among the staff has been found to be helpful for new consultants. Knowing the names of all the staff members, their roles, and how they interact with each other can be very informative and useful for understanding the school culture, and thus helpful in establishing a consultant role. Learning the pattern of relationships (e.g., who eats with whom) also is useful information, as is examining where staff and classes are placed in relationship to each other. For example, placement of special education classrooms, bilingual classrooms, and specialists, including counselors and school psychologists, often represents how they are perceived in the school. An interesting example of that is found in Wyner (1991), who reminds us that, given space is often at a premium, especially in urban schools, space allocations "reflect implicit, unvoiced priorities" (p. 99). Her description of the suboptimal placements of English as a Second Language (ESL) teachers indicated clearly their status in a school.

An important aspect of school culture relevant for consultation is the degree of collaboration engaged in by staff. Activity 2.7 references a school collaboration scale (Appendix A) that you can use in the setting where you are consulting. This scale was part of a larger study, and data on the scale and its relationship to consultation outcomes can be found in Vu et al. (2013).

ACTIVITY 2.7 (INDIVIDUAL, GROUP)

Assessing School Climate for Consultation

Using the survey provided in Appendix A, do the following at your practicum site, internship site, or school where you are employed:

1. Complete the survey yourself.
2. Administer the survey to two other individuals at your school. Try to survey staff members with distinct roles (e.g., general education teacher, special education teacher, school psychologist, nurse).
3. Reflect in writing and/or discussion on what the data suggest about your school's climate:

   a. What results were *surprising* or *unsurprising* to you? Why?
   b. What are implications of the data for your enacting a consultant role at this site?

What Do We Mean by Entry?

We now move on to the concept of entry, the process of the consultant entering and being accepted into the culture of a system or organization, in this case, a school. Effective consultants, whether internal or external to the system, must do two things: (1) learn about the norms and regularities of the school that comprise its culture, which we have discussed previously; and (2) make entry into the school as a professional who seeks to include consultation in his or her scope of practice. Simply walking in the door and greeting the staff is not sufficient as an entry process.

Entering the School as a Consultant: The Entry Process

One of us (SR) was recently asked the following question (only slightly modified for clarity):

We are curious to hear from you on what advice you have for us going out into our internship year. During class time lecture and instruction, we are taught best practice by using the Response to Intervention (RtI) framework. But many of our internship sites are not yet utilizing it, and/or are struggling to implement it. Would you be willing to share your thoughts on how best we as soon-to-be interns can implement and successfully use instructional consultation? Thank you for taking the time to read this email; we hope to hear back from you soon!

Basically, these two interns were asking how to enter a school to be able to provide consultation services, given that most schools do not expect the school psychologist to include much consultation within their scope of practice or perhaps even have clear ideas of what consultation services might look like. They were also acknowledging that what they were taught as best practice in their training might not be in place in the schools. In a focus group interview, an experienced intern supervisor noted that his interns came with many new ideas but did not have the skill to introduce them to the school setting in which they were placed.

For consultation to become a norm within a particular school, the teachers and other staff members need to understand what engaging in consultation, no matter the model, requires of them, and to accept the role of consultee. This introduction needs to happen at two levels: (1) entry into the school as a practitioner expecting to do consultation as part of regular service delivery; and (2) contracting with a specific staff member who is seeking support either for a student or for herself in her professional role. We will come back to the second, that is, contracting, in Chapter 6.

Sarason and his colleagues (1966) recognized the need for a Port of Entry presentation when an external consultant entered a school to provide consultation services. However, an internal consultant (i.e., an individual such as a school counselor or school psychologist, who works in the setting) also needs to assess how and where to enter a school as a consultant, presenting a service delivery model that may or may not be new to the staff. Engaging with the principal, who is the legitimate leader of the school (big rule: never blindside a principal), to ensure that she knows about the intended consultation service delivery to determine the level of support, or, to build support, is an important first step. It is also possible, for consultants who feel less experienced and wish to begin small, to find a responsive teacher with whom to practice together the roles of consultant and consultee around a concern. Sometimes a brief introduction at the first faculty meeting, followed later by a more extensive presentation, will work best, especially if there are some teachers in the room who have experienced success with the consultant or teams.

In beginning her career as a school psychologist, Carner (1982), recognizing the potential to move to a broader role, described her process to restructure a school psychology position in which consultation would be foundational rather than peripheral. She concluded that "there can be a great deal of latitude in creating a consultative role in school psychology—and, moreover, that it is up to the psychologist to demonstrate what is possible" (p. 9). She made her case in her hiring interview, developed an understanding of school culture, worked with the principals, and spoke at faculty meetings—all part of her entry into the schools as a consultant.

In his book about the school psychology internship, Newman (2013) highlighted several key actions interns can take in entering their internship sites, which are summarized and applied to school consultation in Table 2.1. These strategies are relevant for graduate students entering schools as practicum students or interns but also might be useful for early career and experienced practitioners who are entering a new building and wish to incorporate a consultation framework in their practice.

TABLE 2.1 Actions to Support the Consultation Entry Process in a New Setting

Action	Examples of Actions
Be proactive	• Learn about the school's existing regularities and potential entry points for consultation services. • Get out of your office whenever possible and spend time in classrooms; provide direct support to teachers. • Engage in self-assessment and set goals related to consultation knowledge development and skill application. • Work with supervisors to make sure opportunities for consultation are available.
Walk around the school and meet people	• Introduce yourself to teachers and other staff members during orientation, before kids begin; let teachers know that you are available to consult about student concerns. • Send an email, or place a letter in staff mailboxes, introducing yourself and the services you provide, including consultation. • Print out a staff list and write down notes about the new people you are meeting (e.g., personal information learned in establishing rapport; professional needs for support articulated).
Ask questions	• Ask clarifying questions if you are unsure of a school policy, procedure, or terminology. • Asking clarifying questions to students, teachers, and other staff members may unveil hidden regularities in the school culture that might impact your ability to provide consultative services.
Move beyond comfort zones	• Engage in school consultation even if it is new to you and outside of your comfort zone. • Seek out supports such as mentoring and supervision, including observation and feedback, especially if you have had limited school consultation training.

Dr. Lauren Kaiser, as an intern, was able to introduce consultation to her school. Here is her view of how she was able to do so.

However, no matter how the process is introduced at the school level, a teacher receiving consultation services needs to be provided the opportunity for informed consent to engage in the process. Several case studies (see, e.g., Carner, 1982) also confirm that individual teachers don't have a clear understanding of consultation from general presentations made at faculty meetings. Our discussion of contracting in Chapter 6 will provide information on the content and process of contracting to enable consultees to make an informed decision to commit to consultation. But first, we need to discuss two related concepts: building relationships with consultees and developing effective communication skills. When working with a consultee, content is only one aspect of an effective consultant's toolbox. The following two chapters are designed to help you build the skills you will need in those critical domains.

3

CONSULTATION RELATIONSHIPS

Building Working Relationships

Human relationships are not rocket science—they are far, far more complicated.
(James Pennebaker)

We can easily acknowledge that consultation is a helping relationship, but helping is not a simple concept. Perhaps Silverstein (1974, p. 101) put it most succinctly in his poem:

> And some kind of help
> Is the kind of help
> That helping's all about
> And some kind of help
> Is the kind of help
> We all can do without.

Before we explore the complexities of relationships in consultation, consider these questions:

ACTIVITY 3.1 (INDIVIDUAL)

Warm-Up Questions: Relationships

Write down responses to the following questions. You can write sentences or just key words.

1. What does it mean to have a working relationship with a consultee?
2. How does a consultation relationship differ from a therapy relationship? A personal relationship?

3. What assumptions do you have about teachers seeking help from consultants in schools?
4. What is the relationship of trust to building a working relationship?
5. What have you noticed so far about the help-seeking efforts of teachers at your practicum or internship site? What are implications for engaging in consultation?

The relationship is core to the success of any helping process such as consultation, although Schein (2009) suggests that there is still much to be learned about the nature of that relationship. Much of the literature about consultation focuses on the problem-solving process, but we believe that the essence of consultation begins with the establishment of a solid working relationship, one that is perceived by the consultee as helpful. In providing help, there must be understanding and trust:

> Understanding is needed for the helper to know when to offer help and what would be helpful if asked for help. Trust is needed for the client to reveal what is the real problem, to be able to accept what is offered, and to implement whatever resolution might come out of the conversation with the helper.
>
> *(Schein, 2009, p. x)*

Let's begin by differentiating the working relationship from a personal or friendly relationship. Although there can be personal and friendly aspects to a working relationship, sometimes friendly relationships get in the way of working relationships. As one consultant commented, she needed to focus less on being liked and more on getting down to what needed to be done. Sometimes novice consultants work to build a personal relationship; but when a problem in the process occurs or there is a difference in perspective, they discover they do not have a working relationship with the consultee and are unable to productively move the problem-solving forward. In one such case, the consultant-in-training (CIT) did not even attempt to move forward in the problem-solving process with a teacher because she had become so sympathetic to personal issues impacting the teacher, which meant the student referred did not receive the support he needed. Although one consultation relationship between a CIT and a teacher eventually led to their marriage (well after the consultation case was over), in another case a female CIT needed to receive supervisory support on coping with a male teacher who was obviously interested in a personal relationship that she did not want to encourage. With support, she was able to build a working relationship in this situation and provide a successful outcome for the teacher and his students.

Nor is consultation a therapeutic relationship (Sandoval, 2014). Personal issues of the consultee are not the focus—the *work* of the consultee is. When personal issues arise in the process, it is best to acknowledge and move on, or to help the consultee receive an appropriate referral. The key point is that a relationship between two or more individuals can take many directions.

Schein (2009) provides a different kind of distinction about relationships, suggesting that there are three ways that a consultant can offer help, although we can shift back and forth among them: we can be an expert resource to provide information or services; we can diagnose problems and prescribe solutions; or we can be a process consultant who builds a non-hierarchical relationship that begins by clarifying the kind of help that is needed. At times, all of these forms of help can be relevant, but we argue that it is this third kind of helping relationship that school consultants should embrace for maximum effectiveness.

Expert Versus Collaborative Relationship

Over many years, there have been discussions about the distinction between expert and collaborative relationships in the consultation literature (see, e.g., Erchul et al., 2014, for a discussion of this literature). Consultation relationships were seen as either collaborative, that is, two or more professionals, each with their own areas of expertise, working in a nonhierarchical relationship to resolve a problem—more like Schein's (2009) process consultant; or as expert, in which the consultant's expertise is the source of the consultee's acceptance of what the consultant has to offer—similar to Schein's first two roles.

Of course, one should view the expert-collaborative dimension as a continuum, but it is helpful to be aware of where one is on the continuum and if that is the right place. Collaboration has been seen as a way for school consultants to produce change by partnering with the consultee in a way to minimize resistance (Erchul et al., 2014) and enhance acceptance and implementation of interventions, since in most instances, school personnel, aside from administrators, do not have formal or legitimate power over one another. For the expert consultant engaged in a relationship with another school professional, too often the expectation is that the consultant's unique knowledge base will provide solutions that will resolve problems—the expert providing resources. Our confidence or belief in interventions, particularly those that are "evidence-based" according to our literature, seems self-evident to many consultants—but often not to our consultees.

Richard Thaler and Daniel Kahneman both won Nobel Prizes for their work on people's propensity for acting in irrational ways, challenging the belief that people always behave rationally even when it might be in their own interest. Therefore, even if you think you have the correct solution to a consultee's problem, he or she might not accept the solution you have to offer. Or, maybe the consultee's perspective (e.g., about why a solution is not acceptable) is rational in ways that we need to explore more deeply through our communication skills. When interventions do not get implemented or do not work as expected, the reputation of the consultants as experts suffers, and their impact on future problem-solving efforts is at risk. So, it is imperative to focus our thinking on how to influence our consultees other than simply telling them what we know to be best, moving away from the expert and diagnostic-prescriptive roles as often as possible. Rather than call the teacher resistant, the consultant needs to explore these relationship alternatives instead.

Social Influence/Interpersonal Influence

Given that consultation is an indirect service delivery model, the consultant's ability to influence the behavior of consultees through an interpersonal influence process is crucial (Erchul, Grissom, Getty, & Bennett, 2014). As school consultants, our role is to influence our consultees, a truth that sometimes is uncomfortable for new consultants. Erchul et al. (2014) acknowledge that "power and influence are integral to all human relationships" (p. 350). There is a research base in the consultation literature around the kind of social power bases that consultants bring to the process; that is, how consultants can influence their consultees to change in some way, whether it is their beliefs about a problem or student, their attitude toward a situation, or their behavior. An updated list of 14 social power bases has emerged and been studied in a number of organizational settings, including schools (Erchul et al., 2014). However, according to Erchul et al., "no social power base research has documented a clear impact on client behavior change in consultation, thereby currently limiting the contributions of this research perspective" (p. 363). Activity 3.2 defines the social power bases and provides an opportunity for readers to consider their relevance in school culture as well as in consultation interactions.

ACTIVITY 3.2 (INDIVIDUAL, GROUP)

Power in the Consultation Relationship (Adapted from Erchul et al., 2014)

1. Review the definitions of the social power bases, below.
2. For each of the original categories of power (Expert, Referent, Reward, Coercive, Information, and Legitimate), provide an example in the far right column of a time you have used or observed the power used in your school setting. The example can be from any power dynamic/relationship in the school (e.g., principal-teacher; teacher-students; school psychologist-parent); it does not have to be an example of power in consultation.

After providing examples, reflect on the following:

3. What types of power do you believe effective consultants use in a consultative relationship?

4. Can a consultant use more than one type of power in a consultative relationship?

Social Power Bases: Original Categories	Updated Social Power Bases (Raven, 1992, 1993 as cited in Erchul et al., 2014)	Definition in the Context of Consultation	Example of Social Power
1. Expert Power	Positive Expert	Consultee does something because consultant is perceived to be an expert in a particular area	1.
	Negative Expert	Consultee does the opposite because consultee thinks that consultant is thinking of his/her own best interests	
2. Referent Power	Positive Referent	Consultee does something because consultee wants to be similar to or associated with consultant	2.
	Negative Referent	Consultee does the opposite because consultee does not want to be similar to or associated with consultant	
3. Reward Power	Impersonal Reward	Consultee does something because consultee perceives consultant will provide a tangible reward	3.
	Personal Reward	Consultee does something because consultee believes consultant will then like or approve of consultee	
4. Coercive Power	Impersonal Coercion	Consultee does something because consultee perceives that consultant will tangibly punish him/her if not done	4.
	Personal Coercion	Consultee does something because consultee believes consultant won't like consultee if not done	
5. Informational Power	Direct Information	Consultee does something because the information provided by the consultant is perceived to be valuable	5.
	Indirect Information	Consultee does something because consultee heard that the action worked well in a similar situation	

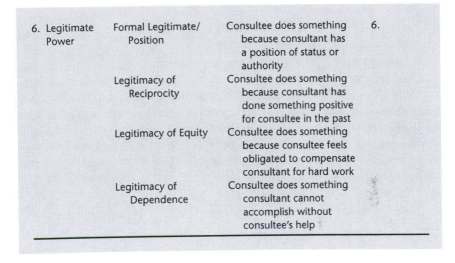

6. Legitimate Power	Formal Legitimate/ Position	Consultee does something because consultant has a position of status or authority	6.
	Legitimacy of Reciprocity	Consultee does something because consultant has done something positive for consultee in the past	
	Legitimacy of Equity	Consultee does something because consultee feels obligated to compensate consultant for hard work	
	Legitimacy of Dependence	Consultee does something consultant cannot accomplish without consultee's help	

The Perils of One-Down Status Position in the Relationship

Developing a collaborative relationship in a helping situation is not simple. In all relationships, there are issues of status positioning; that is, our desire to have the status and position we feel we deserve (Schein, 2009). There is agreement that in most helping relationships, there is a power differential where the helper is perceived as one-up over the helpee. After all, who has the problem, and who has been called in to help resolve it? In essence, there are professional costs to asking for help.

There are multiple examples of specific costs to the consultee who is being helped (Rosenfield, 1987). First, school staff members are busy, and it is difficult to ask for help from a busy professional. An unintended message sent by the busy staff member is that he is too overloaded to take the time to help, which does not encourage asking for help. Key to being approached for help is that the school consultant develops relationships that convey the message of availability for consultation.

It is also important to provide information to school staff, both in faculty meetings, memos, and personally, that using the consultant's services is appropriate and within the scope of services provided by the consultant. This is most crucial when beginning work in a school where collaboration and helping are not part of the school culture. For example, one early career school psychologist struggled to incorporate a consultation-oriented role because staff members were used to the psychologist role being focused on special education decision-making, the emphasis of her recently retired predecessor. Beyond role expectations, in American schools there is a long-standing tradition of praising teacher self-reliance, as we noted in an earlier chapter. Recent changes in school norms to more collaborative relationships need to be encouraged and not necessarily assumed (Rosenfield, Newell, Zwolski, & Beneshek, 2018). Examining your school culture to assess if norms of collaboration and helping are valued will help you to address issues of teacher autonomy as they arise.

Third, help seekers may be perceived and may perceive themselves as less competent. Both helpers and those asking for help enter a relationship with a belief about their own value, and how the relationship evolves depends in part on how much the consultee "grants value to the helper and the degree to which the helper grants value to the [consultee]" (Schein, 2009, p. 14). Consultants who are trying to form collaborative relationships need to be authentic in their respect for classroom teachers requesting consultation. Teaching is a very difficult job, and consultants need to develop an appreciation for the complexities of managing a classroom of diverse students with mixed entry-level skills, motivation, and academic histories, in a context in which there is considerable lack of respect for the teaching profession, often limited support, and high accountability. Appreciating the very human need of the consultee to save face is critical to the success of the relationship.

Trust

Given the critical need to save face in any helping relationship, both by the consultant and the consultee, there must be a sense of trust between them. In this context, trust means: "that no matter what we choose to reveal about our thoughts, feelings, or intentions, the other person will not belittle us, make us look bad, or take advantage of what we have said" (Schein, 2009, p. 18). The consultee will often not reveal what is really going on until trust is established. Here is where our relationship factors come into play, including our communication skills, our ability to convey a sense of interest in the other person, our nonverbal behavior, and our capacity to listen, as described in Chapter 4. Allowing a teacher to be vulnerable about her professional skills, rather than placing the burden for the problem on the student, requires trust. At the most basic level, "trust means safety for our self esteem" (Schein, 2009, p. 19).

Being trustworthy also requires keeping time and other commitments. One simple but critical behavior to build and establish trust is being on time for appointments or having a way to communicate with the consultee when a problem doing that arises. Fulfilling task commitments is also essential, such as doing what you said you would do before the next consultation meeting. Even if the teacher does not follow through on her commitments, the consultant is still obliged to do so.

However, the consultant also can expect the teacher to be there for appointments and to follow through on tasks. When that is not happening, it is important to discuss the reasons and perhaps re-contract on expectations for both parties to the relationship (see Chapter 6). Missing appointments and failure to follow through on tasks are signs that the relationship is not mutually satisfying and requires an open discussion. Sometimes that means that the teacher does not want to continue the relationship, or the tasks are either not meaningful or practical from the teacher's perspective. These are important signs and not to be dismissed as resistance but as relationship issues that require openness and communication.

The Peril of One-Up Status in the Relationship

There are also perils to the one-up status position of the helper, including multiple traps that the one-up relationship can generate for the consultant (Rosenfield, 1987; Schein, 2009). First, until trust is built, the consultee may not be comfortable sharing the real problem. As a result, to protect the teacher's sense of efficacy, the initial focus of the first concern the teacher brings to the table is often a student deficit or problem rather than any issue of instruction or management in the classroom. If the consultant moves too quickly to an intervention on the first problem presented by the consultee, it is not likely to be successful if the intervention does not address the real problem. This issue is often exacerbated on problem-solving teams, where the teacher's self-efficacy is at risk in front of multiple colleagues. In addition, many problem-solving teams allow only a brief period for identifying the problem and move quickly to intervention without sufficient analysis of the problem itself. Even an evidence-based intervention is ineffective if it is used for the wrong problem.

Second, once the consultee has shared a problem, there is often a sense that it is now the consultant's job to resolve it. Consultees often feel as if they have handed over the problem to the consultant for action once the concern has been shared. The pull to solve the problem is strong, and many CITs have been surprised, when listening retrospectively to recordings of consultation sessions, to hear themselves suggesting solutions well before there is a clear delineation of the problem.

Further, the process of giving intervention suggestions must be carefully done, as telling someone what to do maintains a one-up status position for the consultant and a one-down status position for the consultee. In medicine, for example, as much as 30 percent of medication prescriptions go unfilled, and approximately 50 percent of medications for chronic disease are not taken as prescribed (Viswanathan et al., 2012). Glaucoma patients have been found to go blind because they do not use the prescribed eye drops.

The intervention suggestion might also be something the consultee already tried, and the consultee may find it condescending (e.g., "Of course I've tried moving her seat!"). If the initial intervention is not useful or practical, the consultant also risks being seen as irrelevant or not a credible source of support. Relatedly, sometimes the consultee does not want help but validation for her perspective, reassurance that she is doing everything that needs to be done, or just an opportunity to vent about the issues. For example, Guva (2004) makes the case for the importance of understanding why the consultee has come to the consultant, rather than assuming they are asking for help. Sometimes, she says, they are handing over a question (what do we need to do to get this student assessed for special education?), or a task (a request for direct services, such as counseling), or communicating "the *feeling* that something has to be done" (italics in original; p. 256).

In Video 3.1, Dr. Kate Cramer discusses some of the skills in communication and the process of contracting, the first stage of problem-solving, which are helpful in building the relationship. We will be moving on to these skills in future chapters.

Knowing Oneself

Novice consultants may not be comfortable seeing themselves as involved in an interpersonal influence process, but the consultant's role is to help bring about change. We need to develop the skills to support change, and our relationship with the consultee is part of that helping process. Engaging in a relationship that supports change requires us to be clear about who we are.

One key issue that concerns CITs, especially those who do not have much professional experience or lack school experience, is their own competence, or specifically, their competence at their new professional role. Stone, Patton, and Heen (1999) reflect on the core identity issues that often underlie our difficulty in professional conversations and list the issue of competence as critical. As one CIT said, "I know that the more confident and professional I act, the more successful I can be." In our experience, CITs often back off from authentic conversations with consultees because they feel incompetent in the face of teacher expertise, believing they have no power or expertise to create change. Their non-verbal behavior and communication reflect this assumption, a disservice to the consultee who likely perceives this feeling. The same CIT, reflecting on a case that had gone well, made it clear that acting professionally "really had a positive impact." Although she was a novice, she "acted as if" she were a professional, and "it worked."

Learning to trust the power of the consultation process is one way to address this issue. It is helpful for the novice consultant to reflect on and understand the usefulness of the consultation process when it is conducted with integrity. We often recommend that at the beginning, CITs *act as if* they trust the process.

In addition, novice consultants have also used their lack of expertise in the content of the concern to ask authentic and open questions about curriculum, instruction, or behavior management; these "naïve questions" (Garmston & Wellman, 2009) enable the teacher to exhibit her own sense of competence rather than having it called into question because of the request for assistance, and often have led to a more open discussion of the problem. Naïve questions act to lower consultee defenses but also can help to make sure that the consultant and consultee have the same information to move forward in problem-solving.

Having clarity about your own sense of identity can also be helpful to your work as a consultant. The following exercise can be done individually, with some of your classmates, or within a class.

ACTIVITY 3.3 (INDIVIDUAL, GROUP)

Circles of Identity (Adapted from Laidley, Bambino, McIntyre, Quate, & Quinn, 2001)

Think about your "circles of identity" and create one for yourself (see example below). These are (a) descriptors or words that shape who you are and interact with the world, and (b) descriptors or words that other people use to identify you.

Questions for Reflection:

1. With which descriptors do you identify most strongly? Why?
2. With which descriptors do others identify you most strongly? How do you feel about that?
3. Describe a time when your perceptions of a child/student's identity caused you to do something that moved her/him forward.
4. Describe a time when your perceptions of a child/student's identity caused you to do something that held her/him back.
5. How does *your* identity, either descriptors you chose or others choose for you, impact who you are as a consultant?

Possible Group Activity:

Get into groups of three (classmates you do not always work with). Look at one question at a time. Take one minute to think. Each partner has one full minute to speak while others listen. If the person finishes speaking before one minute is up, the group should sit in silence. Switch persons at the end of each minute.

Example of a circle of identity:

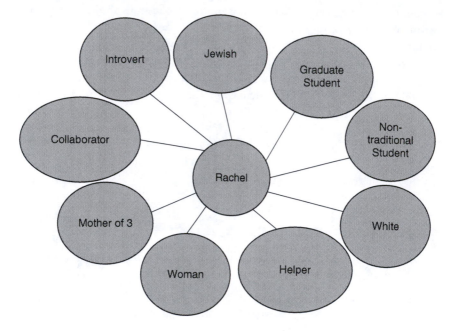

Difficult Conversations Within the Context of a Consultation Relationship

We have introduced one source of tension that can lead to a difficult conversation, that is, whether the consultee is meeting agreed upon commitments. Other sources of tension can arise from different perspectives about issues and practices, such as whether rewarding students is a good practice. Teachers often resist rewarding student behavior, which the empirical literature supports, because they believe it should not be necessary to do so. The discrepancy between the teacher's perspective and the literature can provide a barrier to a consultant's objectivity with a teacher who pushes against a practice that is supported in the research. There is a tendency in such situations to simply repeat what the research says over and over in different ways, but that will not necessarily change the perspective of the teacher who has her own response to reward.

Stone et al. (1999) stress that all difficult conversations have an underlying structure, which includes:

- what is the situation that calls for the conversation;
- what are the underlying feelings about the situation;
- and, least likely to be acknowledged, what the situation means to our sense of who we are.

ACTIVITY 3.4 (INDIVIDUAL, GROUP)

Unpacking a Difficult Situation

Read the following case example, and then answer the subsequent questions individually. If possible, compare responses with a partner or in a small group

Case Example:

In one case, a teacher was missing appointments on a regular basis but kept promising she would do better; the CIT was reluctant to have a conversation about this situation, and the lack of progress and meeting dragged on.

Questions for Reflection:

1. Using Stone et al.'s (1999) structure, how would you assess the issues in this situation for the consultant?
2. What is the nature of the situation that requires a conversation?
3. What are the underlying feelings that the teacher and the CIT had?
4. What did the situation mean for the consultant?

Stone et al. (1999) invite us to think about intentions that we attribute to our colleagues—what assumptions are we making about the teacher's intentions? Did we assume she wanted to end the relationship? In one case, a teacher's daughter was getting married, and the teacher was frantically trying to attend to all the details while working full time—there was just not enough time to incorporate the consultation meetings into her day. However, the CIT assumed a different intention, that she was not interested in the consultation process. Although it is not always possible, or appropriate, to talk about feelings, sometimes it can be helpful to do so. The teacher in this case had some feelings that needed to be addressed; the feelings of the CIT needed to be addressed as well. The communication skill of perception checking, presented in Chapter 4, can be helpful in discussing feelings that are present but might otherwise go unacknowledged. In many situations, there is a quick tendency to assess blame, especially to label the teacher as "resistant." We need to move from blame to assessing what caused the problem and how we might move forward. In the next chapter, we will introduce the Ladder of Inference, to help understand and unpack the inference-making process.

The third aspect of the Stone et al. (1999) structure has to do with what the issue has to say about one's self. For a CIT, holding a difficult conversation can be especially troubling if the self message is: "I am not doing this consultation thing very well," instead of: "how can I get better at this and learn from this experience while I have good supervision, and maybe I am not seeing this accurately anyway." One CIT expressed it this way:

> Because I was concerned about offending or frustrating Mrs. Smith, I often felt myself attempting to avoid areas that I thought might be sensitive or apologizing to her ... Specifically, I have learned the importance of checking in gently with a teacher regarding her perceptions instead of making assumptions about them ... Additionally, I have learned to make my communications more direct and pointed and then to move on, rather than lingering over sensitive topics in an attempt to soothe or apologize. By being direct and stating my concerns briefly before moving on, I allow the teacher to hear me without creating a prolonged and perhaps difficult conversation about subjects that have already been discussed.

We all have internal doubts when learning a new set of skills, and having the confidence and persistence to move forward can be intimidating, especially in the face of a difficult situation. Perhaps the best advice comes from Stone et al. (1999):

> Instead of wanting to persuade and get your way, you want to understand what has happened from the other person's point of view, explain your point of view, share and understand feeling, and work together to figure out a way to manage the problem going forward ... Changing our stance means inviting the other person into the conversation with us, to help us figure things out ... We need to have a learning conversation.
>
> *(p. 16–17)*

As one CIT expressed it,

> I am learning the importance of developing a sense of confidence in my own competence so that an upset teacher does not in turn upset me. By becoming upset myself, I make it more difficult to communicate in a clear and effective manner that truly addresses what the teacher is saying.

The Helping Relationship

A helping relationship needs to be built—it can't be assumed. It begins with the very first contact between the consultant and potential consultee—perhaps even before, if we consider how the consultant enters the culture of the school. Recognizing that the relationship is unbalanced at the beginning (the one-down status position of the consultee), that trust must be built, that communication matters, and that an open discussion of the process is essential to avoid misunderstanding (likely to occur anyway) will help the consultant to negotiate a productive working relationship. In Chapter 6, we will discuss the importance of the initial contracting session to the process of building the relationship. First, let us explore the communication skills that act as the building blocks of the consultation relationship.

4

COMMUNICATION SKILLS

The single biggest problem in communication is the illusion that it has taken place.
(George Bernard Shaw)

Most of the consultation process takes place through verbal and non-verbal communication between the consultant and consultee. However, the role of these consultation conversations is far more complex than they seem on the surface. Not just simple information sharing, these conversations are:

> dynamic, interactive and inclusive. They evolve and impact the way we connect, engage, interact, and influence others, enabling us to shape reality, mind-sets, events and outcomes in a collaborative way … giving us the exquisite ability to get on the same page with our fellow humans.
>
> *(Glaser, 2014, p. xiii)*

The words we choose and the tone we use, as well as our non-verbal communication, make a difference in the message we intend to convey. Through our interpersonal communication, we obtain and provide content but also sustain the collaborative relationship and build trust.

Communication skills are at the heart of effective consultation, and they are learnable. The goal of this chapter is to begin the process of developing communication skills that will support and enhance your consultation experiences. Consultants-in-training (CITs) who listen to their recorded consultation sessions are often surprised at what they actually said and how they said it, versus what they intended to communicate. In this chapter, we will discuss several techniques and how they are useful to you as a CIT, as well as give you the opportunity to practice and reflect on your emerging communication skills. To begin, reflect on the role of communication in school consultation in Activity 4.1.

ACTIVITY 4.1 (INDIVIDUAL)

Warm-Up Questions: Communication Skills

Write down responses to the following questions. You can write sentences or just key words.

1. How do you use communication skills to move a collaborative process of problem-solving forward?
2. What are some principles of collaborative communication that will guide your work as a school consultant?

The Power of Words

Consultation is fundamentally a conversation between the consultant and the consultee. It is often difficult for us to understand that "language does not so much reflect reality as create it" (Watzlawick, 1978, p. 16), a phenomenon that has a long history in psychology and the other helping professions, even though it may be new to many consultants. For example, family therapists (e.g., Anderson & Goolishian, 1988) have long recognized that we generate meaning as we interact with each other through language.

Social psychologists have also provided research that supports the importance of language and communication in consultation. Higgins and his colleagues (1999) have researched the way verbal interactions actually shape reality for the communicators:

1. Audience Tuning: We modify our message to take into account our perceptions about what our listener wants to hear. When speaking to a school psychologist about a potential referral, our consultees may think school psychologists or counselors want to hear about the possibility of and evidence to suggest a disability.
2. Shared Reality: Talking about a topic with another person generates beliefs about the objectivity of the message. So, if our consultee teachers talk about a potential learning disability, they may become even more convinced about the certainty of that diagnosis. In one school, grade-level teacher teams that had discussed student issues and decided the specific students had disabilities were less open to the school-based prereferral team's suggestions for classroom interventions (Benn, 2004).
3. Correspondence Bias: There is a tendency to see the person rather than the situation as the source of behavior. School consultants often struggle to help teachers understand the importance of their own instruction and management strategies in student problem behavior rather than continue to embrace the assumption that the students have a deficit unrelated to the classroom context.

You will see these and other communication issues arise as you work in the schools as a consultant.

Communication Strategies

There are specific communication strategies that will support your work as a consultant. We often hear graduate educators and CITs comment that the communication skills they learned in counseling are the same ones we use in consultation; however, there are subtle differences in how these skills are used in consultation. In this chapter, the following communication skills will be discussed: listening and its challenges; obtaining information, including the art of questioning and clarifying; paraphrasing to ensure you understood the speaker; perception checking when affect is involved; and the bond and move strategy when applying more than one skill will be more effective.

It is critical for you to record your consultation sessions since reflecting on the communication skills you use is essential for the development of your own competence in consultation. We will provide some exercises for you to practice these skills, but deliberate practice requires you to reflect on your actual communication behavior in the context of a consultation session, preferably with feedback from a supervisor.

Listening

Michael Francis, conductor of The Florida Orchestra, claims that when we listen together, we come together. While he was talking of the power of music, we will consider how this also applies to the power of listening to each other. He also contrasts listening with hearing. Just hearing is not enough. Hearing is so automatic that we often do not realize how difficult it is to listen accurately and effectively in a consultation session, nor how much what we hear is shaped by our own thoughts as we listen. CITs practicing listening skills often comment that it is hard work, as it is an active, not a passive, process. Although you often find the term *active listening* to label such responses as eye contact, facial expressions, nodding, "yes," and "uh-huh," they are just a subcategory of listening skills, although certainly they support the perception of the consultant as attentive and involved during the session.

Strategies to Address Typical Listening Challenges

Here are several common challenges that you will need to be prepared to address as a competent listener.

Develop Awareness of How Often We Jump to Conclusions/Make False Inferences

From research on memory, we know that we don't register communication by others as if we were audio-recording the words. We hear the message filtered through our own biases and perspective (see, e.g., Roediger III, Watson, McDermott, & Gallo, 2001). We remember something as having been said when it was only inferred, since we continue to make multiple inferences during our conversations with others (Roediger III et al., 2001).

A useful concept to keep in mind is the power of the Ladder of Inference (Argyris, Putnam, & Smith, 1985; Senge, Klewiner, Roberts, Ross, & Smith, 1994), that is, our propensity to reach conclusions without really thinking through how we got there. This reflexive loop moves us from observable data and experiences, such a video-recorder might capture, from which we select data, add our own meaning (cultural and personal), make assumptions based on the added meaning, draw conclusions, adopt beliefs, and take actions based on those beliefs. At the bottom of the ladder is *sturdy ground*—observable and measurable behaviors for problem-solving, and at the top of the ladder is *shaky ground*—inferential conclusions transformed from the initial observation. An example of the Ladder of Inference idea is provided in Figure 4.1.

So, when a teacher comes to you with an initial description of student's problem, you often need to work together with the consultee to move this down the Ladder of Inference to the actual behavior of the student. Activity 4.2 presents an opportunity to consider the Ladder of Inference in action. The figure should be viewed from bottom to top.

Shaky ground: Actions are taken based on assumptions and beliefs rather than data	Irene is referred for a special education evaluation.
Assumptions and beliefs about the world are adopted	"Some students are just beyond my reach, and that's okay. She'll be better off in another setting."
Conclusions are drawn based on personal and cultural meaning added to the data	"She is a student in need of specialized instruction, and belongs in special education."
Assumptions and beliefs are made based on meaning that is added to the data	"There's nothing I can do to help Irene in my classroom. She's too far behind and needs something more than I can give."
Personal and cultural meaning is added to the data	"Mom has some issues, too; the apple does not fall far from the tree."
Data is selected based on observation	"Irene is currently on pace to fail the third grade."
Sturdy ground: Observable and measurable data.	Third-grader Irene is significantly behind peers in reading achievement, despite an evidence-based reading curriculum and Tier 2 intervention. She frequently does not complete classwork or homework. She has inconsistent attendance, and has attended multiple schools since Kindergarten.

FIGURE 4.1   Example of the Ladder of Inference Applied to School Consultation.

ACTIVITY 4.2 (INDIVIDUAL, GROUP)

Ladder of Inference

If you were listening to this statement, draw a possible ladder of inference (see Figure 4.1 for an example of what this might look like). If possible, compare with a partner or in a small group.

> **Teacher Consultee:** Guess I expect some support in the area of suggestions of how to make some changes in his daily behavior. He challenges me and he is so impulsive consistently that I need some suggestions. It doesn't seem like the things I've been able to use over the years that were quick fixes seem to work with him. And perhaps additional testing needs to be done with him for behavior or academic reasons.

Develop the Confidence to Listen to the Speaker Rather Than Plan Your Next Response

Particularly neophytes in consultation often are planning what they are going to say next, rather than focusing on what the consultee is saying. Staying with the consultee's own words is often the key to moving the dialogue forward, rather than moving on to our own next question. We will come back to that as we discuss the power of clarification responses. Using the same transcribed excerpt that you reflected on in the context of the Ladder of Inference activity, consider what aspects of the teacher's statement would be helpful to clarify further.

ACTIVITY 4.3 (INDIVIDUAL, GROUP)

Identifying Points of Clarification

Review this excerpt from a real teacher consultee. Underline those aspects of what the consultee stated that you think require further clarification. Then answer the subsequent question individually and, if possible, compare response with a partner or in a small group.

> **Teacher Consultee:** Guess I expect some support in the area of suggestions of how to make some changes in his daily behavior. He challenges me and he is so impulsive consistently that I need some suggestions. It doesn't seem like the things I've been able to use over the years that were quick fixes seem to work with him. And perhaps additional testing needs to be done with him for behavior or academic reasons.

Question:

Why did you underline what you did as requiring further clarification?

Focus on Non-Verbal Cues in the Consultee and Yourself

Words are only part of what need your attention as a listener. So much is communicated non-verbally; if you don't attend to that, you will miss the opportunity to really *listen to* what your consultee is saying. In one case, a CIT was busy taking notes and missed the point at which the teacher moved back in her seat in response to a question, indicating her concern about what the CIT was asking. As the CIT viewed the video recording, she recognized this non-verbal movement as an indication that the topic was sensitive to the teacher, which helped the CIT in the next session to check in with the teacher consultee about it.

Additionally, your own body language provides messages to the consultee, sometimes unintended. For example, frequent head nodding demonstrates active listening but may also inadvertently suggest agreement even when you do not agree with what the consultee stated. Or looking down at your notes may suggest a lack of listening to the consultee, when in reality you are just trying to keep an accurate record of what the consultee has said.

Avoid Glossing Over Emotional Tone

If anger or frustration is part of a consultee's message, avoiding it in your responses will suggest to the consultee that you have not really listened to the message being conveyed. For CITs, this is a common challenge because they are eager to move forward in solving the problem or want to avoid getting involved in emotional interactions. However, clarifying that you have heard the feelings being expressed confirms the depth of your listening; often you are able to respectfully acknowledge the consultee's emotions, and in the same response, move on by seeking additional clarification about the problem at hand. We explore potential consultant responses to emotional tone later, in a section on perception checking.

Become Adept at Courteous Interrupting

Consultees often have a lot to share, and sometimes you may feel awkward or rude speaking up when the consultee is speaking. However, being a good listener sometimes requires interjecting to ensure you understand the consultee's experience of the problem. As described by Caplan (1970):

> I sit beside the consultee, actually or metaphorically, and I involve him in questioning the material he presents about the case. I do not allow the consultee to talk for more than a few minutes without interrupting him with questions. I avoid, under all circumstances, a situation in which I listen in relative silence while the consultee tells a long story about the client and turns to me at the end and says, "What do you think about it and what should I do?" First, I probably will not know what he should do. Second, since I may not yet know what the elements in the story really mean to the consultee, I will not wish to say something the inner meaning of which to the consultee I will not know.
>
> *(pp. 85–86)*

Here is an activity for you to consider about when and how to interrupt.

ACTIVITY 4.4 (INDIVIDUAL, GROUP)

Interrupting the Consultee

Answer the subsequent questions individually and, if possible, compare responses with a partner or in a small group.

1. How comfortable would you be interrupting a consultee? Why?
2. Given the following transcript dialogue, at what point would you interrupt?

Teacher Consultee: He's doing everything. Messing around in his seat, dropping his pencil, getting up to get Kleenex, moving around, and turning on the fan. Everything but his work. I can get a need to walk around. A lot of kids with ADHD need their outlets, or kids with hyperactivity just need to do something physical. I get that. But a lot of the things he does aren't channeled, whether it's yelling out across the classroom, insulting other students, or falling over in his seat. Sometimes he does do the class clown behavior. A lot of students around him find it annoying because they are trying to do their work. And they'll say, "Scotty, stop it!" That's when he retorts and says, "Shut up, you're an idiot." He'll take any type of comments from his classmates as negative even if they are trying to do something that's positive. Luckily I have a pretty good class first and second period, so really they see him as not being a good role model, whereas other classes will see that as clowning and follow along with it. Not the class I currently have. They will say, "stop it," and that sets him off. It's an anger issue. Often times if you try and correct him without explicitly reasoning with him, and it's something he can't entirely understand, he gets angry about it. For example, if I want him to move to the back of the class because he is disrupting other students, he will object to it. Whether it's throwing little fits, saying, "I don't want to do it," flat-out refusing to do it. If you don't word it exactly right to him and be like, "Scotty, you are having a little trouble right now, and I don't want you to get in trouble for these things you are doing. Do you think sitting in back will help?" If you don't word it exactly right with him, he takes it negatively, just like he takes the attention from his classmates negatively.

Obtaining Information

Every consultee brings a concern framed in a story that they tell to the consultant. Working with the consultee to develop a narrative that leads to change in perspective or to a potential solution is the goal of communication. Listening is only one part of the work. Now let us turn to the other side of the listening/speaking communication cycle—how we gain the information needed to support the change from problem to solution. We will begin with the skills required for the art and science of obtaining information for problem-solving, including, but not exclusively, question asking.

The Art of Questioning

Making sure the *right* problem is found is not as simple as asking direct questions. Berger (2014) found that successful problem-solvers "were exceptionally good at asking questions" (p. 1). In fact, he views good questions as ones that often lead to unexpected and productive answers. His concept of a beautiful question is one "that can begin to shift the way we perceive or think about something—and that might serve as a catalyst to bring about change" (p. 8). That is very similar to Hylander's (2004, 2012) concept of a *turning* in consultation, a conceptual change in the consultee brought about by the consultation process. She and her colleagues developed a set of questions for preschool staff to help them explore the meaning of student behavior from the consultee's perspective in such a way as to shift their perspective.

For example, in exploring issues around anger in preschool settings, Michelsen (2004) discusses the impact of introducing a surprising question. She asks the consultee a comparative gender question: *if he had been a girl? Or, if she had been a boy?* This question helped to widen the frame of reference and "to increase further reflections, consciousness, and emotional and cognitive understanding of anger in girls and boys and the consultee's interactions with angry children" (p. 296). Exploring how questions can be used to shift how a problem is seen is a critical skill to learn.

Schein (2013) views good questions as ones that also help to build positive relationships. In a diverse world, we need to ask questions based on mutual respect, recognizing that our consultees know things that are needed to be known in order to solve problems. He finds that too often consultees know things that are critical to resolving a problem but that are not expressed because consultants do not listen, do not take the consultee's knowledge seriously, or simply do not ask the right questions. He recommends "humble inquiry," specifically, "the fine art of drawing someone out, of asking questions to which you do not already know the answer, of building a relationship based on curiosity and interest in the other person" (p. 2).

Our goal in this chapter is to provide you with some support in learning to ask the right questions.

Who Asks the Questions?

If the consultant comes to the *Problem Identification and Problem Analysis* (*PID/PA*) interview with the belief that she should be asking the questions and the consultee providing answers, she risks creating an identified problem that is hers, one to which she believes she can provide answers. For example, if the consultant who is a school psychologist moves the problem toward the possibility of a disability, then she has the instruments to conduct a diagnostic examination. If the consultant knows little about academic content and instruction, then her questions can avoid exploring that area even if the teacher mentions such an issue. In reviewing transcripts of consultation sessions, teachers often suggest the presence of academic issues as well as behavioral ones; but CITs with more comfort in the behavioral area and without knowledge in the academic domain often fail to follow up on these concerns, focusing instead on the behavioral ones, maintaining the expertise of the consultant to identify and address the problem. Activity 4.5 presents such a choice point.

ACTIVITY 4.5 (INDIVIDUAL, GROUP)

Consultant Question Focus

In the following quote from an actual consultation meeting, what would your next question be? Write down a response and, if possible, compare with a partner.

Teacher Consultee: Well, in phonics, for example, some days he would put all three sounds together, other days he knows the sounds and he can't put them together. He doesn't try.

Consultant Response:

Using the Consultee's Own Words to Explore the Problem: The Clarifying Question

Consultees provide us with information about the concern that they want us to address, but it is often an error to assume that we have fully understood the problem without seeking clarification of their presentation. Remember the concept of the Ladder of Inference (Argyris et al., 1985; Senge et al., 1994)! Much of our *understanding* comes from what we fill in from the conversation, because large sections of what is said by consultees in referral interviews are either unclear or open to multiple interpretations. Some typical examples of problem statements include words such as: *immature, poor attention span, doesn't complete work, no discipline.* See Table 4.1 for more examples of high inference language that is commonly heard in schools. By bringing your attention to these words, we hope that you will help consultees move down the Ladder of Inferences through clarification and also consider the clarity of your own language in problem-solving.

There are multiple ways to request clarification, not all of them even questions. Here are some starter sentences to help you to request clarification:

- Can you give me an example?
- I am not sure I understand what you just said.
- Tell me more about that.
- What behavior do you see that leads you to consider him immature?
- What is the work he is not completing?

TABLE 4.1 Examples of Red Flag Words

ADHD	Lost
All day long	Low achiever/performer
All the kids	Naughty
All the time	Never
Always	None of the kids
Anxious	No number sense
Asocial	On the spectrum
Aspergery	Parents don't care
Disorganized	Rough home life
Disrespectful	Rude
Doesn't stop	Sassy
He just struggles	Simple
Her parents don't care	Slow processer
Hyperactive	Sluggish pace
Lacks attention	Space cadet
Lazy	Unmotivated

Other Types of Questions

It is important to differentiate clarification from other types of questions. In fact, asking relevant questions when seeking to understand what brought a teacher to the consultation process is the most common strategy. Too many consultants work from a script of questions, while we see the value of building from the consultee's own words as they describe the problem.

Expert-oriented consultants see their goal as obtaining information about "the problem" from the consultee. So after sometimes allowing the consultee to vent about the situation, consultants will pose a series of questions in which they obtain the information that they want to know. Such a process places the consultant squarely in the expert mode, and according to Dillon (1979), there are some negative consequences of this questioning process:

> Far from encouraging client expressiveness, questions are held to produce blocking, to reduce input, to cut off conversation, and to inhibit response ... In answering the questions, the client will reveal the information requested, but expressions of problems, feelings, relevant facts, and other data pertinent to understanding the ... situation will not be forthcoming ... Questions ... generally, cause him/her to settle into a passive acquiescent role, or at worst, they provoke a sense of threat, resistance, and defensiveness.
>
> *(p. 76)*

As we have been suggesting, it is essential for consultants to recognize that they are often selective about what they choose to address, which then influences the direction and focus of the *PID/PA* process. Return to Activity 4.5 as you review the following paragraph. You had some choices here, which is often true in actual consultation sessions. You could focus on the child's behavior (In what kinds of situations do you see him not trying?), or you could clarify (What do you mean by not try?), which would take you in one direction, or you could focus on his phonics skills (Let's talk about his phonics skills. What sounds does he know and what does he not know?). In this actual case, not trying was the key issue for the teacher, but the lack of vowel knowledge turned out to be the core problem.

Of course, some questions are not relevant to resolving a concern. Sometimes consultants ask questions about the student's family that are not helpful in resolving the classroom problem. Knotek (2003) examined several such instances in problem-solving teams, such as when team members discussed family living arrangements rather than the student issues in the classroom, to the detriment of problem-solving efforts.

To focus on the difference between types of questions, Activity 4.6 will provide you with some practice exercises.

ACTIVITY 4.6 (INDIVIDUAL, GROUP)

Clarifying, Relevant, and Irrelevant Questions

1. Individually, write down a response for each of these three excerpts.
2. If possible, compare your responses with a partner. Determine if your question is clarifying, relevant, or irrelevant. How do you know?
3. If possible, as a whole class, share examples of each with your classmates.

Excerpt 1:

CIT: Have you ever been involved in any type of problem-solving approaches before?

Teacher Consultee (TC): Probably, but not with that designated name.

CIT:

Excerpt 2:

TC: The particular student that I have some concerns about, his daily work is not up to speed, and I feel like he can be doing a better job on his daily work, and I need to know what I can do to help him improve his daily work score.

CIT:

Excerpt 3:

TC: He's very distractible and prefers to try to change to subjects that are completely off-topic to what is going on in the classroom.

CIT:

Making Sure You Understood: The Art of Paraphrasing

It is often an incorrect assumption that you understood the consultee until you confirm that. By paraphrasing, you are essentially testing your own understanding of the message. For example, if the teacher consultee says, *James does not comprehend what he reads*, what does the teacher actually mean here? Is it a comprehension problem? Or is there an underlying decoding skill or language issue? Rather than assuming it is a comprehension problem, it is important to first assure the teacher that you heard what she said. This is the skill of paraphrasing.

A paraphrase does not merely repeat what was said, but checks your own understanding by trying to restate the teacher's words with your own words. It is your best attempt to comprehend what the consultee said and to then restate the meaning in your own words. Returning again to the teacher consultee quote we previously considered, now think about the use of paraphrasing in this example.

ACTIVITY 4.7 (INDIVIDUAL, GROUP)

Paraphrasing Practice

Review this excerpt from a real teacher consultee. Consider how you might respond to this teacher's statement with a paraphrase and write your response below. If possible, compare your responses with a partner.

Teacher Consultee: Guess I expect some support in the area of suggestions of how to make some changes in his daily behavior. He challenges me and he is so impulsive consistently that I need some suggestions. It doesn't seem like the things I've been able to use over the years that were quick fixes seem to work with him. And perhaps additional testing needs to be done with him for behavior or academic reasons.

Consultant:

Paraphrasing may not be enough of a response, and we will return to this later in the chapter.

Responding to Affect: Perception Checking

Maintaining a collaborative relationship requires also understanding not only the consultee's content, for which you might use a paraphrase or ask for a clarification, but also being open to understanding the consultee's feelings that may be expressed, sometimes by words and sometimes by non-verbal means. You may perceive that there is an emotion but need to consider two issues: (1) how to acknowledge the emotion, and (2) whether your perception is accurate.

Just as in paraphrasing, where you need to confirm that your perception of the content is accurate, in perception checking, you validate that your perception of the feelings is accurate. Perception checking is restating the feelings you think are present, in your own words. You may not be correct, but you then give the consultee the opportunity to correct your understanding. It should be done in a nonjudgmental way and in an even tone.

> **Teacher Consultee**: Today Drew was really bad. Like, he wouldn't do anything … it took him 45 minutes to come to the rug because he was playing with a piece of string. He keeps picking things off the ground, and I can't be monitoring him all the time and making sure there isn't a piece of paper on the ground.
>
> **CIT**: Oh wow, that seems frustrating. It sounds like you have your hands full. Was there anything that he did well today?

In this example, the CIT perception checked and used the bond and move strategy, to be discussed next, after the perception check to reorient the teacher to working on the problem.

CITs sometimes express their concern that it is inappropriate to discuss consultee feelings in a task-oriented problem-solving process. They sometimes fear that they will open a Pandora's box of feelings. But here the goal is clear communication, not therapy. Consultation is, by its very nature, interpersonal, and attitudes, emotions, and expectations are part of the data gathering. Consultees have very human emotions, which the student's behavior or the teacher's feelings of helplessness can engender.

Also, we are not always rational about our experiences and our reactions. As Bersoff and Grieger (1971) so eloquently stated, "At times, … teacher concerns about a child's behavior may be based on irrational attitudes and ideas that lead to irrational expectations, demands, and feelings, and inappropriate actions toward the child" who exhibits problem behavior (p. 484). Misunderstanding the feelings that you perceive the consultee is expressing may lead to inferences that are inaccurate and short-circuit an interaction, so it is important to perception check. Moreover, assessing if there are hidden agendas related to feelings can provide information about where the problem is and what interventions will be accepted. There is a difference, for example, between frustration and anger, which would lead a good consultant to move ahead in different directions. Moreover, a good perception check at the very least can tell the consultee that you want to understand the feelings.

Bond and Move

As we have been suggesting, often it is not enough to paraphrase or perception check, especially if the consultee's statement is ambiguous to begin with, as it was in the activity dialogue above. Combining communication strategies can be even more powerful in moving the problem-solving process along. In the bond and move strategy (Rosenfield, 2012), it is recommended that after paraphrasing or perception checking as a way to demonstrate that the consultee is being heard, the consultant can then move on to obtain additional information, perhaps through clarification. So, for example, after letting the teacher know that you heard she is concerned about the student's comprehension skills, you can clarify just what she means by asking for an example or a request for further information about the student's comprehension.

Developing Awareness of Cultural Communication Styles

Ingraham (2014, 2017) provides a window into "how one's communication style can impact their consultation effectiveness" (p. 302). She cites Hall's (1976) concept of *context communication,* specifically differentiating cultures with "high context (where extensive knowledge of the culture is needed to interpret meaning of communications) and low context (where the message is straightforward and does not necessitate knowledge of the culture to infer meaning)" (p. 302). While her concern is particularly important for consultants working in the global arena, it also has relevance for those within a particular culture. She encourages consultants to learn about their own communication style preferences and their intersection with consultees using different communication styles.

In Video 4.1, Dr. Colette Ingraham integrates her perspective on multicultural consultation with the communication skills we have been presenting earlier in this chapter, such as questioning.

One of the communication styles that Ingraham (2017) addresses in her training is understanding the difference between direct and indirect communication styles. She has found that "affective reactions of people when they encounter a style divergent from their own can be intense and can jeopardize relationships and consultation" (p. 302). Sometimes it is also true that a consultant and consultee using the same communication style can be unaware of how that interferes with making progress in problem-solving. In one case, both members of the consultation dyad used indirect communication styles and made little progress in their sessions (Newman, 2012).

A similar cultural communication issue has been described in the work of Tannen (2007, 2017) on gender differences in communication styles. She describes both the unique communication pattern of women as well as the differences between men and women in communication style, describing the often invisible influence of gender conversational style. Although it is important to point out that not all of us conform to our typical gender communication patterns, it is useful to be aware of the potential for misunderstanding if differences are not considered. For example, she has found evidence that women will talk about a problem or concern to gain understanding or support, whereas men will be prompt to provide advice when a problem is described. Recall Guva's (2004) paradox presented in the last chapter, namely that teacher consultees do not always ask for help when they ask for consultation: sometimes they are handing "over the *feeling* that 'something has to be done'" (italics in original; p. 256). This can lead to an example of admiring *the problem* rather than focusing on problem-solving. We will see this issue raised again in Chapter 7, within the *PID/PA* process.

Additional Activities for Practice

We have included in Activity 4.8 an abridged transcript for you to reflect on a CIT's communication skills in action. We have also included a Process Log format (Appendix B) to assist you in reflecting on transcriptions of your own actual consultation recordings. Finally, Activity 4.9 provides an opportunity to reflect on your own use of communication skills in action. The tool provided in Activity 4.9 could also be used for observing someone else consulting, whether in person (i.e., real or simulated), on video, or while reading a transcript. These activities do not substitute for examining your communication skills in context, but they will provide you with some experience in reflecting on how you communicate.

ACTIVITY 4.8 (INDIVIDUAL, GROUP)

Transcript Reflection

The following is an actual excerpt from the second *Problem Identification/ Problem Analysis* session of a CIT's consultation session with a first-year, second grade teacher. Read the transcript, and answer the subsequent questions individually and, if possible, compare responses with a partner or in a small group.

> **Teacher Consultee (TC):** Spelling he's okay ... it's more structural ... getting an actual complete sentence out. I mean, you have that writing sample ... I mean, he's not horrible, he's definitely lacking some skill sets...
>
> **CIT:** But would you say that your priority would be to actually get him to start writing, or...?
>
> **TC:** Definitely. Because honestly, I don't care if his words are spelled wrong, as long as he's writing, I think that will help him.
>
> **CIT:** Alright, well that's good to know. One of the things today, when I was talking to him (following a classroom observation), he wasn't so clear with the directions. Was that something that you have found with him—that it takes more than one time to explain the directions?

TC: Definitely. I think, though, even when you do take the time to explain it, and also, the people... I purposely put him with Jesse and Alisha because they're very strong in reading and writing, and they'll try to help him.

CIT: They gave him an A-plus on his paper (referring to a mark they wrote on his paper that morning) (laughs)

TC: (laughs) Yeah, they'll try to help him, and sometimes he doesn't want the help, so. I don't know how much it is another way to get out of it. Maybe he doesn't understand it, and some things if he really doesn't understand, I don't know...

CIT: So you're saying when he doesn't want the help, he's trying to avoid it still?

TC: Like he'll go, "I don't understand," and they'll try to explain it to him, and he just will totally ignore them and not listen.

CIT: Mm-hm, I see. So when I wrote, "difficulty with writing," I think we can be more specific and say, "with actually producing words." What do you think?

TC: Yeah, definitely. Forming complete thoughts and sentences.

CIT: So, writing complete thoughts and sentences. What do you mean when you say "complete thoughts and sentences"?

TC: Sometimes in his writing, he'll just... I can just remember what we were writing about... we were writing about: "What's special about you?" and he has this bling-bling necklace... and instead of writing, "My necklace makes me special," he'll just write, "Necklace." It's not like a complete thought or something like that.

CIT: So, if we were to look at his production, it's more important that it would be a complete sentence, not necessarily like, "He wrote 30 words..."

TC: Yep.

CIT: But you're not worried about spelling or grammar.

TC: Nope.

CIT: Okay. Now, today would you prefer to focus on reading or writing stuff? Where is your gut telling you?

TC: I think writing. He's doing better in reading. I think writing.

CIT: Just one thought that I had with reading—which is an off the cuff thing—when he had this spare time to pick a book from the library, the book that he was reading, he brought over to read with me, which I thought was adorable, but, it was something that was really hard for him, I felt like, the book that he was reading. Maybe something that would be helpful for him at that time to keep him on task is if he had a book selection that was a J or below, of books that were at his benchmark level.

TC: Maybe it was because up there in the back there are books that are benchmarked. But they usually like reading hard books (laughs).

CIT: Yeah, and then sometimes he's reading the hard one and gets up and moves around and stuff because he can't really read it.

TC: Yeah.

CIT: So in terms of his, like right now, his writing, can we look at his journal again and maybe get an idea... we can either use that as a baseline for how much he's actually producing, or we could do it another way....

TC: That's fine. Because journal I do every single day, so that would be a good way to see... (looks in student's desk for his journal) you can see his library books... He took out Harry Potter. I mean (laughs)... that's not really his level.

CIT: Yeah, one of the things that I talk about in my class a lot is the idea of practicing, of relevant practice, and you know, as he's learning new words, if he's reading something with those words in it where it's easy for him to read, that would be helpful.

TC: So, Harry Potter might not be that helpful (laughs).

CIT: (Laughs) He's awfully ambitious!

Questions for Reflection:

1. Identify what communication skills the CIT used during this session (when applicable, write the skills in the left margin of the transcript).
2. What did the CIT do well?
3. What could the CIT have done differently? If you would have responded differently, write what you would have said next to the teacher's response.

ACTIVITY 4.9 (INDIVIDUAL, GROUP)

Communication Skills Reflection Tool (Adapted from Gravois, Gickling, & Rosenfield, 2011)

Transcribe part or all of a recording of a consultation session with a teacher. Reflect on the consultant's use of communication skills by using the format provided below and responding to the subsequent questions. Note that this tool could also be used for self-assessment of your own communication skills or for observing another consultant's communication skills. It is also a helpful way to provide critical feedback to a peer or a supervisee.

Communication Skill	Tally of Occurrence	Examples	
		Consultant Statement	Consultee Response
Active Listening			
Clarifying Question			
Request for Clarification not in the form of a question			
Paraphrase			
Perception Check			
Bond and Move (Paraphrase or perception check combined with another communication skill)			
Offering Information			

Questions for Reflection:

1. What communication skills did the consultant apply well? How do you know? (Hint: The consultee's response often provides important information.)
2. What communication skills need improvement? How do you know? (Hint: The consultee's response often provides important information.)
3. Identify alternative responses for any interactions you believe need improvement.

5

THE CONSULTATIVE PROBLEM-SOLVING PROCESS

An Introduction

Trust the Process

In schools, most consultation services begin with someone having a problem or a concern that calls for additional support or a desire for collaboration. The problem-solving process has, in fact, been adapted into the schools, both in direct service through behavior analysis models and in indirect models of consultation. Before further overviewing the problem-solving process, take a moment to reflect on your own assumptions regarding this process in Activity 5.1.

ACTIVITY 5.1 (INDIVIDUAL)

Warm-Up Questions: The Consultative Problem-Solving Process

Write down responses to the following questions. You can write sentences or just key words.

1. Problem-solving is described as a *systematic* process. What do you think this means?
2. What do you think are the consultant's roles and responsibilities during the problem-solving process? What about the consultee's roles and responsibilities?

In the School Consultation (SC) model we have developed here, the process begins with an understanding of the context (school culture), a commitment to building relationships with consultees, and developing effective communication skills to be used during the problem-solving stages in order to enable the consultant and consultee to have a more productive experience. We now move on to the problem-solving process.

Dr. Janet Graden describes the application of a problem-solving process in schools and its relationship to SC in Video 5.1.

It is imperative to stress that effective problem-solving is not an informal process. According to D'Zurilla and Goldfried (1971), applied psychologists adopted problem-solving methods from basic research and theoretical literature, as those methods came to be viewed as having real-life relevance. Many problem situations are complex, ambiguous, or have conflicting demands, making obvious or usual solutions often ineffective. Student concerns fit this pattern of *messy* real-world problems, where the information needed was not obvious and the directions for solving them were unclear to those working with them. D'Zurilla and Goldfried stressed the importance of inhibiting the impulse to respond quickly to solve the problem, when it was actually important to define the situation in operational terms and distinguish relevant from irrelevant information, identify primary goals, and specify the issues and conflicts. As we shall see, this is the very purpose of the critical initial Problem Identification and Problem Analysis stage we will be presenting in Chapter 7.

The benefits of problem-solving also include that the process *"(a) makes available a variety of potentially effective response alternatives for dealing with the problematic situation and (b) increases the probability of selecting the most effective response from among these various alternatives"* (italics in original; D'Zurilla & Goldfried, 1971, p. 108), which we will explore in Chapter 8, in the section on intervention planning. However, D'Zurilla and Goldfried (1971) also sounded a warning: most people do not approach problems systematically without training. So our purpose in the following chapters is to present the skills necessary for effective, systematic problem-solving and to help you to develop those skills through activities.

The SC model is clearly structured as a stage-based process, originally described by D'Zurilla and Goldfried (1971). At its appropriate implementation, the process holds the consultant and consultee accountable for the outcome. The chapters that follow provide a step-wise view of the stages of problem-solving in the SC model. All prevalent models of problem-solving consultation follow similar stages of problem-solving, with overlapping work to be accomplished within these stages (Kratochwill, Altschaefl, & Bice-Urbach, 2014). Irrespective of model, these questions are answered during consultative problem-solving:

What is the problem (Problem Identification)?
Why is it happening (Problem Analysis)?
What can we do about it (Intervention)?
Is the intervention working (Evaluation)?

The SC problem-solving stages we define here build specifically upon two consultation models: Behavioral Consultation (BC; Bergan, 1977; Kratochwill & Bergan, 1990; Martens, DiGennaro Reed, & Magnuson, 2014) and Instructional Consultation (IC; Rosenfield et al., 2014). We have illustrated how SC compares to BC and IC in Table 5.1. We have also included rationales for our alternatives to traditional BC and IC stage names and features. In Table 5.2, we overview the components of each SC problem-solving stage in depth. The features of each stage are largely informed by Gravois, Gickling, and Rosenfield's (2011) *Training in Instructional Consultation, Assessment, and Teaming*. All of the stages and stage components of BC are subsumed within the SC stages. Our purposes in reworking this process are: (a) to further clarify the stages, and (b) to account for the relationship variable in consultation (Rosenfield, 1991).

Moving on to the Stages

In the following chapters, we will introduce each of the stages and provide you with information on the process as well as activities to support your development of knowledge and skills. In Appendix C, we provide a tool to measure adherence to the SC problem-solving stages. This tool can be used for self-assessment while reviewing your own recording of a consultation meeting or to assess another consultant's adherence to the SC process.

TABLE 5.1 The Problem-Solving Process in School Consultation, Behavioral Consultation, and Instructional Consultation

School Consultation (SC)	Behavioral Consultation (BC)	Instructional Consultation (IC)	Summary and Rationale of Differences of SC and BC	Summary and Rationale of Differences of SC and IC
1. Contracting	—	1. Contracting	Additional stage because: • SC views a consultant's understanding of school culture as a prerequisite for effective consultation; this is learned during entry, and discussed with the consultee during contracting • SC is embedded with distinct assumptions which are clarified up front during contracting • Contracting accounts for the initiation of the consultation relationship with clear relational expectation	No differences
2. Problem Identification and Analysis	1. Problem Identification 2. Problem Analysis, including Treatment Design	2. Problem identification and analysis, including Instructional Assessment	Stages are combined because: • Treatment design not considered part of problem analysis • Problem identification and problem analysis occur concurrently in practice • Identifying and defining the problem precedes intervention planning	Instructional Assessment is part of this stage, as well as other stages of problem-solving, but the full training process is beyond the scope of this text. Readers are referred to Gickling, Gravois, and Angell (2016) for an extensive treatment of Instructional Assessment

3. Intervention Planning	—	3. Intervention Planning	• Stage separated from BC's Problem Analysis stage to be a distinct stage because "intervention planning is a distinct process • "Treatment" re-termed "intervention" because "treatment" implies a medical model while "intervention" does not	• No differences
4. Intervention Implementation, Monitoring, and Performance Feedback	3. Treatment Implementation 4. Treatment Evaluation	4. Intervention Implementation, including Evaluation	• Stages are combined because intervention implementation and evaluation occur concurrently in practice • "Treatment" re-termed "intervention" because "treatment" implies a medical model while "intervention" does not • "Monitoring" added to stage because progress monitoring is a common term in contemporary educational practice • "Performance feedback" added to stage because performance feedback is a research-based component of school consultation practice	• "Monitoring" added to stage because progress monitoring is a common term in contemporary educational practice • "Performance feedback" added to stage because performance feedback is a research-based component of school consultation practice

(continued)

TABLE 5.1 *Continued*

School Consultation (SC)	*Behavioral Consultation (BC)*	*Instructional Consultation (IC)*	*Summary and Rationale of Differences of SC and BC*	*Summary and Rationale of Differences of SC and IC*
5. Post-Intervention Planning and Closure	——	1. Resolution/Termination	Stage separated from BC's Treatment Evaluation stage to be a distinct stage because: • Post-intervention planning is a distinct process, including planning for generalization and maintenance of behaviors • Post-intervention planning includes redefining the consultant–consultee relationship	"Resolution/termination" re-termed "Post-Intervention Planning and Closure" because: • The consultation relationship might continue after a case closes • The consultant and consultee plan for intervention fading, behavioral maintenance, and/or generalization as part of case closure

TABLE 5.2 An Overview of School Consultation Problem-Solving Stages (Adapted from Gravois, Gickling, & Rosenfield, 2011)

Stage	Purpose	Business to be Accomplished
Contracting	• Introduce consultee to the school consultation model, including assumptions, expectations, and process • Gain agreement to work together	• Discuss consultee expectations and prior experiences consulting • Introduce the school consultation assumptions, expectations, and process • Explain stage-based problem-solving process • Clarify school as the context for problem-solving, including the concept of instructional match • Explain potential application of problem-solving for at multiple tiers in addition to individual students • Clarify shared ownership of the problem and the consultation process • Clarify non-evaluative nature of the consultation process (only if true) • Explain the parameters of confidentiality • Check for consultee agreement and commitment to participate • Schedule follow-up meeting/ ongoing schedule
Problem Identification and Problem Analysis	• Create shared perception of consultee concerns • Define problem in observable and measurable terms • Establish baseline of current performance • Establish goals	• Create shared understanding of consultee's concern(s) using collaborative communication skills • Define concern(s) in observable terms • Define concern in the context of the school/classroom, and consider the role of instructional match/ mismatch • Follow up with additional data collection such as record or work sample review, observation, or instructional assessment • Prioritize concerns • Establish a plan to measure current performance (i.e., Baseline) • Establish baseline measurement of performance • Set performance goals based on baseline data

(continued)

TABLE 5.2 Continued

Stage	Purpose	Business to be Accomplished
Intervention Planning	• Collaboratively develop instructional and/or behavioral management strategies targeting goals	• Elicit consultee's ideas/strategies • Discuss: *What* classroom-based strategy will meet goals? *Where* will strategy be implemented? *When* can strategy be implemented? *How often* will strategy be implemented? *Who* will be responsible? • Consider conditions to create/maintain instructional match • Consider if multiple students can benefit from the intervention • Document specifics of what, when, how often, and who
Intervention Implementation, Monitoring, and Performance Feedback	• Ensure intervention adherence/accurate implementation of intervention	• Continue meeting while intervention is being implemented • Clarify what's working and what needs refining • Elicit consultee's perception of progress • Provide performance feedback regarding level of adherence to intervention, with consideration given to implementation changes as needed • Collaboratively review and discuss data • Compare progress with goals
Post-Intervention Planning and Closure	• Formally conclude the consultation relationship regarding the targeted concern	• Close if (a) goals are met; (b) consultee can implement independently if needed; (c) strategies are fading/faded • Elicit consultee's plans to maintain student progress • Determine documentation of efforts • Consider addressing other priority areas not yet addressed (and return to PID/PA for new priority concern) • If case is explicitly closed, let consultee know how support can be accessed in the future • Communicate with parents, colleagues, teams as needed

6

CONTRACTING

Making the Invisible Visible

It takes both sides to build a bridge.

(*Fredrik Nael*)

The School Consultation (SC) problem-solving process begins with *Contracting*, when an agreement, usually verbal, between the consultee and the consultant is reached that makes the process of consultation transparent to the consultee. It is essential that the consultee have the opportunity to provide informed consent to participating in the process. Transpiring *prior to* tackling problems, contracting is a systematic process through which consultation assumptions and expectations are explicitly discussed, so that the consultee (or consultees—the process can include more than one consultee) can make an informed decision regarding entering the consultation process. The process of contracting should not be so overly rigid as to stifle the relationship but, at a minimum, a verbal discussion of expectations for the consultation should occur and should include the consultee's verbal agreement to work with the consultant on the concern. When contracting is neglected or components of contracting are ignored, challenges detrimental to problem-solving may subsequently arise. In contrast, when implemented well, contracting serves as the foundation of trust and honesty on which the consultation relationship and successful problem-solving efforts are built.

In this chapter we consider (a) the *necessity* of establishing a consultation contract; (b) the *content* that should be included in a consultation contract; and (c) *process* issues related to effectively contracting. As in other chapters, multiple real examples of contracting interactions are provided along with activities, allowing you to learn and practice this stage of problem-solving. We will spend considerable time on this stage, as understanding contracting will also familiarize you with the subsequent problem-solving stages themselves. Before further exploring the components and process of contracting, take a moment to complete Activity 6.1.

ACTIVITY 6.1 (INDIVIDUAL)

Warm-Up Questions: Contracting

Write down responses to the following questions. You can write sentences or just key words.

1. In what ways do you think the contracting stage of problem-solving relates to school culture?
2. In what ways do you think the contracting stage of problem-solving relates to building relationships?
3. Why do you suppose it is important for the consultant and consultee to clarify their expectations prior to beginning a consultation case?
4. What should a consultant do if a consultee does not wish to proceed in working together in the consultation process?

Why a Consultation Contract Is Necessary

Consistent with our definition of competent consultation in the introduction to the text, contracting adds some structure to informing how a consultant *talks* to someone about a problem. The consultee's *informed consent* to participate in consultation is obtained via contracting and is likely to enhance the effectiveness and satisfaction of consultants and consultees (Thomas, 2010). In a recent study synthesizing data from 38 qualitative consultation research studies, data from 12 of the studies suggested that a combination of understanding school/organizational culture (i.e., processes of entry) and establishing clear expectations and procedures for consultation (i.e., process of contracting) made positive differences for how consultation relationships developed and problem-solving ensued (Newman, McKenney, Silva, Clare, Salmon, & Jackson, 2017). Several examples from Rosenfield's (2012) compilation of school consultation case studies also evidenced the importance of contracting; for example, Pas (2012) demonstrated, as explored later in this chapter, that when expectations of the consultation process are unclear, it may negatively impact the problem-solving process.

Consultation contracts are embedded within the contexts of psychological contracts and visible contracts (APA, 2017). Psychological contracts are *invisible* expectations regarding work obligations, efforts, and remuneration. Norms and regularities of school culture, in addition to individual preferences, affect implicit role expectations, such as how a school consultant's work schedule is divided (e.g., time engaged in assessment vs. time engaged in consultation) and how much responsibility a teacher owns for supporting students outside of school hours. *Visible contracts* are written/signed contracts between employers and employees. They explicitly specify salaries, hours, and other job expectations. External school consultants might sign a written contract with a school for their work. However, internal consultants and consultees do not often sign a written contract; therefore, expectations for the consultation process, relationship, and roles can by default become *implicit unless there is a specific process to clarify them.*

Thus, the *consultation contract* offers an opportunity for the consultation dyad to begin problem-solving with *explicit*, clear assumptions, expectations, and roles. In other words, the *invisible* expectations hidden in psychological contracts and school culture can become *visible although not written down as with visible contracts.* The contract should be negotiated with the person who brings the problem to the table and who will be responsible for carrying out any planned interventions (Conoley & Conoley, 1992); sometimes this involves more than one person.

If there is misalignment between the consultant's and consultee's assumptions or expectations, this is best clarified before problem-solving begins. Here is an activity that demonstrates the value of a consultation contract.

ACTIVITY 6.2 (INDIVIDUAL, GROUP)

Clarifying Expectations Early in Consultation

Read the following example. Answer the subsequent questions individually and, if possible, compare responses with a partner or in a small group.

Imagine you start consulting on a case for a first-grade student named Yusaf. You believe consultative problem-solving efforts will support Yusaf's reading fluency and comprehension in the general education classroom. The teacher believes that Yusaf has a learning disability requiring intervention support outside of the general education setting and that the purpose of consultation is to document Yusaf's need for specialized instruction.

Questions for Reflection:

1. What are the implications of this misalignment of assumptions?
2. How might clarifying expectations up front support more effective consultative problem-solving?
3. What else would you want to consider about the teacher's expectations for consultation?

The Nuts and Bolts of Contracting

The SC Model of consultation described in this text has embedded assumptions, as listed in Table 6.1, that are clarified during the contracting stage of problem-solving. A checklist for contracting with these components, as well as examples of how these may be discussed in contracting, is provided in Figure 6.1. In short, contracting provides an opportunity for you to introduce the assumptions, expectations, and process of SC.

Previous Consultee Experience With Consultation

However, before you offer too much information, it is advisable to inquire about the consultee's prior experiences and expectations. Information provided by the consultee may contrast with your own assumptions and expectations as a school consultant. For example, many consultees have primarily engaged in *on the fly* consultations, been on the receiving end of advice without feeling their perspectives were taken into account, or engaged in storytelling about students or families without really problem-solving. Unearthing such prior experiences can stimulate an excellent introduction to how this consultation process will be similar and different. Activity 6.3 provides an additional opportunity for you to think about how you might approach discussing prior experiences when consulting with a teacher.

TABLE 6.1 An Overview of the Contracting Stage of Problem-Solving

Stage	*Purpose*	*Business to Be Accomplished*
Contracting	• Introduce consultee to the school consultation model, including assumptions, expectations, and process • Gain agreement to work together	• Discuss consultee expectations and prior experiences consulting • Introduce the school consultation assumptions, expectations, and process • Explain stage-based problem-solving process • Clarify school as the context for problem-solving, including the concept of instructional match • Explain potential application of problem-solving at multiple tiers in addition to individual students • Clarify shared ownership of the problem and the consultation process • Clarify non-evaluative nature of the consultation process (only if true) • Explain the parameters of confidentiality • Check for consultee agreement and commitment to participate • Schedule follow-up meeting/ongoing schedule

Contracting Task	Example of Language	Observation (Tally and/or Comment)
☐ Discuss consultee's expectations, prior experiences	"What expectations do you have for our work together?" "Tell me about what prior experiences you have had consulting/problem-solving."	
☐ Explain stage-based problem-solving process	"The stages of problem-solving include…" "The problem-identification and analysis stage will be the 'heavy lifting' for us, so we're sure to intervene on the correct problem"	
☐ Clarify school as the context for problem-solving, including concept of instructional match in problem-solving	"By attending to instructional match, we'll consider the fit of the student and her prior knowledge with the instruction in the classroom, and expected tasks"	
☐ Explain potential application for other students	"Sometimes we find that other students can benefit from the intervention we are working on for one student"	
☐ Introduce the collaborative consultation process	"In this process we will work shoulder-to-shoulder through a series of steps to identify, define, and intervene on concerns"	
☐ Clarify shared ownership of problem and process	"We will co-construct the problem, and work step by step together to solve it"	
☐ Clarify non-evaluative nature of process (only if true)	"This is a non-evaluative process – none of the information will be shared with the principal, or be connected to evaluation of your performance"	
☐ Explain parameters of confidentiality	"This process is confidential – we will not need to share what we are working on except…(with the team, with the students' parents, etc.)"	
☐ Check for agreement/commitment to participate	"Does this sound like a process you'd like to work on together?"	
☐ Schedule follow-up meeting/ongoing schedule	"When would be a workable, regular time for us to meet?"	

FIGURE 6.1 Checklist for Contracting in Consultation.

ACTIVITY 6.3

Contracting Transcript: Prior Experiences Consulting Example 1

The following is an excerpt from an actual contracting session between a consult-ant and consultee. Review the transcript and answer the subsequent questions individually and, if possible, compare responses with a partner or in a small group.

> **Consultant (C)**: Tell me about your prior experiences with consultation
>
> **Teacher Consultee (TC)**: It was very sporadic and different being in the city because they don't have the same services that are availa-ble at this school. It was a team-based approach... the caseworker would come in and observe before the whole team got together. Or sometimes the school psychologist would come in and do an observation. I had a behavior checklist that I had to fill out, and one was sent home to parents to fill out as well to see if the behaviors were consistent across school and home. That's what I remember.
>
> **C**: Ok ... was it that you were working with somebody or was it that each person had his or her own part to do?
>
> **TC**: Each person had their own part to do, and then the team would meet and come up with the plan that would work ... it was more so only done when it had to do with Special Education.

Questions for Reflection:

1. How might the consultee's prior experiences influence her expectations of the current consultation process?
2. Imagine you are the consultant. Use the following sentence starters to (a) paraphrase the consultee's prior experiences, and (b) contrast those experiences to what she might expect in her work with you:

   a. "It sounds like your previous experiences with consultation included..."
   b. "Our process will look a bit different. We'll..."

Description of Consultation Process

As you get a sense of the consultee's prior experiences and expectations, you can also offer information about your own experiences, assumptions, and expecta-tions. For example, you'll want to clarify that consultation is an indirect, col-laborative, and systematic process with specific stages. Problem-solving should be described without using too much jargon. Laundry listing the problem-solving stages or describing stage business in too much detail is likely to *lose* the consultee or inadvertently create a *one-up* power dynamic antithetical to the collaborative dynamic you are trying to establish. The consultee should be clear that the process is ongoing and will involve meeting on multiple occasions over time. Sandoval (2014) suggests that the consultant make it clear that an immediate solution will not be provided until sufficient information is obtained, referencing the importance of the *Problem Identification and Problem Analysis (PID/PA)* stage, which alleviates expectations of an expert dynamic.

Given the school-based context of problem-solving, it is important to specify that you are interested in the student's instructional match or the alignment of the student's prior knowledge, the curriculum or task they are engaged in, and the instruction being provided. Doing so makes it clear that this is an ecological rather than child-deficit focused process. It may also be helpful to illustrate the instructional triangle heuristic, originally developed by Bloom (1976) as the learning triangle, for the consultee (see Figure 6.2). We return to the concept of instructional match in Chapter 7.

Also relevant to the school-based context is the assumption that problem-solving is viewed through a multi-student lens, namely that the work the consultee does in the consultation for a single student may actually be relevant for multiple students in the classroom or future students with similar concerns. Multiple students may benefit from assessment strategies and the many interventions that are discussed, and it is helpful to make this possibility explicit to the consultee early in the process. We have not yet considered each of the problem-solving stages in depth, but the information provided in Chapter 5 and here should give you enough information to begin practicing the contracting process.

Discussion of the Collaborative Relationship

It is essential to discuss the nature of collaboration during *Contracting*, as preconceptions of the consulting relationship will vary based on the consultee's prior experiences. During a *Contracting* session, a teacher expressed her concern about previous less-than-positive experiences, particularly when it came to intervention

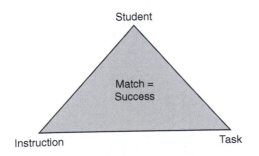

FIGURE 6.2 Instructional Match Triangle.

development. The teacher stated: "It's hard when people are telling you you should do this but there's no way with all the other students that you can possibly do it." The consultant-in-training (CIT) during contracting saw the need to both validate the teacher's frustration but also to indicate that she would work together to create something feasible, knowing that this issue was key to gaining the teacher's trust to engage in the process.

Activity 6.4 provides a contracting excerpt where the dyad discussed the consultee's prior experiences consulting, which revealed some problematic dynamics collaborating with other teachers. As the example demonstrates, a discussion such as this might be an excellent jumping off point to discuss that the relationship will be collaborative and what collaboration will consist of in the context of the relationship (e.g., shared responsibility for exploring and defining problems and planning and implementing interventions; mutual value of the consultee's and consultant's expertise, as both help us to understand the problem).

ACTIVITY 6.4 (INDIVIDUAL, GROUP)

Contracting Transcript: Prior Experiences Consulting Example 2

The following is an excerpt from an actual contracting session between a consultant and consultee. Review the transcript and answer the subsequent questions individually and, if possible, compare responses with a partner or in a small group.

Consultant (C): Have you ever engaged in consultation before?

Teacher Consultee (TC): Well, not with the school psychologist.

C: How about anyone else in the school?

TC: Um, I would not say that it was formal consultation, but I talk to the other fifth grade teachers a lot but most of the time it ends up that we just complain about our students (laughs).

C: So you've had some interactions with the other teachers in fifth grade, but you didn't find much value in your conversations.

TC: Exactly, I am always trying to do new things and get our grade team together, but we always end up just bashing ideas down and we all leave conversations more discouraged than when we started.

C: It sounds like you are really trying to be a leader here. What would be some of the things that you would find value in from consulting with someone?

TC: Well, when you do the same thing day in and day out, year after year, you get stuck in a rut. Each year classes are different, and they should be treated differently. I just feel like I don't know what to do sometimes to help some of my struggling students. It would be nice to hear what other people do or some ideas of what to do.

C: That's great that you are seeking out strategies from others and that you recognize the importance of student differences. Hopefully we can work together and find some things that will work for you in your classroom and for Oliver, but also maybe for some other students.

TC: Great! Finally!

Questions for Reflection:

1. What information does the consultee offer about her prior experiences with collaboration?
   a. What does this suggest about grade-level collaboration?
2. If you were the consultant, how might you use the information provided by the consultee to introduce expectations of the consultation relationship?
3. What might this say about the culture of the school regarding collaboration?

Evaluation and Confidentiality

The topics of evaluation and confidentiality (and limits therein) should be covered during the contracting process. Consultation is presumably a non-evaluative process in which the consultant's role is to support rather than to evaluate the consultee's work performance (e.g., a teacher's instruction or classroom behavior management). A non-evaluative process allows the consultee to ask for assistance; state that something is not working; or acknowledge being stuck without fearing negative consequences, such as receiving a poor performance evaluation or losing a job.

The process being non-evaluative intertwines with it being between the consultant and the consultee to the extent possible; the consultant does not generally share with others what is discussed during consultation interactions unless safety concerns for a student or students should arise, or the process is part of a school problem-solving team. There is no legal confidentiality right for the consultant or consultee. Moreover, the consultee is not held to the same expectations of confidentiality as the consultant (Sandoval, 2014), and is free to discuss the content of the consultation sessions. If the consultation is part of a team problem-solving process, as is true in the Instructional Consultation Model, there should be no expectation of confidentiality, as much of the information is shared with the team. As a CIT, you may be required to audio- or video-record your consultation interactions; if so, when discussing confidentiality, you should be clear about who will listen to recordings (e.g., self, university supervisor, field supervisors, peers in your cohort during peer supervision) and that recordings will be deleted after review.

Although the non-evaluative, confidential, and voluntary aspects of consultation have long been assumed to be part of the process, their precise boundaries have never been complete and have become even more blurred in contemporary consultation practice (Erchul, 2011). For example, an evaluative authority such as a principal may ask you to consult with a teacher, with implications for whether or not the process is truly evaluative, confidential, or voluntary. Problem-solving teams as settings for consultation also do not provide a confidential setting for teachers to share their concerns. With the implementation of Multi-Tiered Systems of Support (MTSS) in schools, a consultee may be expected to share results of consultative problem-solving with a data team and with parents to demonstrate a student's progress in areas of concern. Although some exceptions exist with respect to these features of consultation, the key is being clear and explicit about them up front during contracting. Violations of the contract would undermine trust with the consultee and potentially mitigate your effectiveness as a consultant within the larger system.

Informed Consent

The contracting process concludes with the consultant checking for consultee agreement and commitment to participate in the process. Consultation is a voluntary process, and though it may feel awkward confirming the consultee's readiness to consult when they already had requested your assistance, securing the consultee's informed consent to participate confirms you are on the same page with *how* the consultation process will proceed. Before formally asking for agreement, asking an open-ended question such as: "Before proceeding, what questions do you have?" (in contrast to "Do you have any questions?") may elicit any concerns, such as the time commitment for the process. Finally, you can openly ask the consultee if he or she wants to participate in this process and when would be a good time to meet next.

Once the consultee agrees to participate, it is time to move to the *PID/PA* stage of problem-solving. Often, this happens immediately after confirming agreement to work together. If the consultee does not wish to participate in consultation, that is acceptable, too. Again, the process is voluntary, and consultees may not view the structure as fitting their needs. It is better to know this before the process begins.

Process of Contracting: Tips for Success

Although we offer a checklist of items to discuss during contracting (Figure 6.1), this stage of problem-solving is more nuanced than checking items off of a list. Following are some considerations to promote a successful contracting stage.

Make It a Dialogue

Since you will be offering a lot of information about the problem-solving process, your assumptions, and your expectations, it is easy for contracting to become a monologue. This is in contrast to the communication skills we have discussed thus far and also to the bi-directional nature of the consultation relationship and interactions you are trying to build. As described earlier, asking about the consultee's prior experiences and expectations for consultation begins the process as a discussion. Demonstrate genuine interest and active listening and use the points brought up by the consultee as a starting point to compare or contrast the SC process. For example, a consultant might state:

> **CIT**: It sounds like your grade-level team shares a lot of resources, but you don't always work together when interventions are put in place in your classroom. During our process, we will continue to meet as the intervention is in place to check in about Evan's progress.

Still, the consultant, who has a lot of information to share, may inadvertently dominate the contracting session. Therefore, at times it is useful to stop and make a statement such as, "I've been going on for a while. Let me stop and ask you what questions or thoughts you have about the process I just described?" Doing this will break up the monologue to help make it more of a conversation. In total, the contracting dialogue should be approximately 5 to 10 minutes in length.

Don't Apologize for the Process

It is likely that the teacher you are consulting with has never had someone contract with them prior to consultation or consulted in a systematic way, such as what you are proposing. This leads some CITs to be self-conscious or even apologetic in how they describe the process (e.g., CIT: "We'll work through a formal process, which can be time consuming—sorry about that"). Apologizing for the consultation process before it even begins can undermine your ability to be an effective consultant. Instead, realize that although this process is different than what the consultee (or you) may have experienced in the past, it is structured this way for a reason.

Relatedly, since consultees may not be used to contracting, they might be ready to dive right into *PID/PA* before contracting is complete. We have discussed several of the challenges with glossing over this stage of problem-solving. If a consultee should try to move ahead before the stage is complete, it is okay to demonstrate that you heard the consultee's concern and then refocus back to contracting. For example:

> **CIT**: It sounds like Ellen's been a real handful. I am eager to talk more about your concerns. Before we dive too far into the problem, I just want to make sure we're on the same page about this process. If it's okay with you, can we finish up the contracting discussion before moving to discussing the problem?

Consultant Student Status

For CITs, a frequent concern is that the consultee is working with the CIT as a favor (i.e., helping to get a graduate school assignment completed) rather than genuinely in need of consultation assistance. A CIT reflected this very concern in a supervision process log:

> I think it will be interesting to see how our working relationship develops. Currently, Mrs. King sees me more as a student then as a professional. In our conversation, she kept referring back to how she understands that I need to get my work done, referring to this consultation case, because she remembers what it's like to be a student. So, I am hoping that through my professionalism and working together on this case, our relationship will develop into more of a professional relationship rather than a teacher/student relationship. It may also be necessary to address directly (e.g., "I am a student, but I hope that you find this to be a good use of your time—it is not just for me to complete an assignment.")

This is an issue that can be addressed during contracting by making an explicit statement such as the one proposed by the CIT. Although it is kind of a teacher to use her time to support a graduate student, the process should ultimately be beneficial to the consultee and her students. Even when a consultation starts off as a favor, CITs should bear in mind that, although they are learning to consult, they have more to offer than they might think—especially if they are engaged in ongoing consultation supervision of their work.

Revisiting the Contract

As you are getting to the end of this chapter, we hope that you are thinking that contracting is more involved than you had initially thought. Indeed, there are a number of components of contracting and nuances in how they are discussed with the consultee. Sometimes, consultants forget to discuss something during the contracting stage. Do not fret. Rarely is something missed that cannot be brought up at a later time, for example at the beginning of the next session in an opening summary.

Sometimes, though, even when all the contracting components are covered, a dyad begins the consultation with misaligned assumptions. In a compelling example provided by Pas (2012), the consultee, based on her prior experiences, assumed that Pas would take a prescriptive approach to consultative problem-solving, providing solutions for the consultee to implement. This perspective was inconsistent with Pas' collaborative approach, which had not been sufficiently clarified during contracting. As the consultation progressed, the divergent perspectives became more evident in consultation interactions, which Pas discussed with her consultation instructor/supervisor. Therefore, Pas decided to address the relational dynamic by revisiting the contracting discussion:

> This is actually a good opportunity to revisit some of the stuff that we talked about in the first week. I hear you apologizing to me and feeling badly about [not collecting data] and I am wondering if we can kind of go back to where we quickly skimmed through the process and talk a little bit about our relationship. You don't have to feel bad about this; a really essential part about the type of consultation that I would like to do is a little different from what I understand the IST [instructional support team] process may be like. I don't want this to be an expert mode, like "I'm the boss" and that I will come in and say "this is what you should to do" and if you don't do it that I will [think or say] "That bad teacher didn't collect data." I really want to work—I guess a good phrase is shoulder to shoulder—with you about this concern.
>
> *(Pas, 2012, p. 201)*

Revisiting contracting led to a return to the *PID/PA* stage of problem-solving and subsequent stages, all with additional consultee input.

In addition to misaligned relational expectations, other symptoms may indicate a need to revisit contracting. These include a consultee being frequently late or absent to meetings or distracted in meetings, not adhering to the intervention, presenting with negative verbal or nonverbal behavior, or even talking with you differently when the recording device is off (e.g., "Here's what's really happening...") due to fear of evaluation. In such instances, revisiting relevant aspects of contracting can be useful. For example, for a consultee who seems to have lost interest in meeting with you, inquiring about the behavior can be helpful: "I noticed we haven't been able to get together for a couple of weeks. I just wanted to check in and make sure this process is still something that you want to do." Most often consultees still do want the consultation support and will be responsive to your reminder about the expectations of ongoing meetings. This falls into the category for many CITs as a difficult conversation. And, indeed, sometimes the consultee really does want to stop, as in one case where the teacher's daughter was getting married and the consultee was feeling too overwhelmed to continue meeting with the CIT. Both accepting that and leaving the door open for the future are important to making this a positive experience for both the CIT and the consultee.

We conclude this discussion of contracting with a video demonstrating two doctoral-level CITs from the University of Cincinnati, Amanda Covey and Keisha Hill, engaging in a simulated contracting experience. Activity 6.5 is aligned with Video 6.1 of a contracting session, enabling you to process the session in action.

ACTIVITY 6.5 (INDIVIDUAL, GROUP)

Contracting Video

Watch the video of a consultant and consultee contracting for consultation.

1. Follow along with the contracting checklist (Figure 6.1).
    a. Indicate what components of contracting the consultant completed and what was missed.
    b. Write down phrases the consultant used that you thought were helpful.
2. How did the process of consultation fit with what was described in this chapter?
3. What went well? What would you do differently, if anything?

Additional Activities to Practice Contracting

As with all stages of problem-solving, *Contracting* is best learned through practice with opportunities for feedback. Activity 6.6 is a lab activity intended to help you practice contracting skills in a simulated environment.

ACTIVITY 6.6 (GROUP)

Contracting Lab

1. If possible, in a group of three or four, divide up roles: One or two observers, one consultant, one consultee.
2. The **consultant** should contract for the consultee's agreement to consult with the components of the contracting stage. The practice can be audio- or video-recorded, especially if there is no observer.
3. The **consultee** should act as you think a consultee might in this situation: Curious, agreeable, have sought out assistance in advance, but haven't consulted in this way before. Following the practice session, the consultee should provide this feedback to the consultant:

a. How did it feel to be on the consultee end of contracting? Did it feel conversational or robotic?

4. The **observer(s)** should use the contracting checklist (Figure 6.1) to take notes while observing regarding content and process. Following the practice session, provide this feedback to the consultant:

   a. Was the contracting you observed a monologue or dialogue? What evidence do you have for your argument?

   b. Provide critical feedback in writing, using the checklist, and verbally with examples of consultant statements.

Summary

Consultation is a bi-directional process built on trust and happens *with*, rather than *to*, the consultee. Therefore, a consultee should be able to make an informed decision about whether or not to participate in consultation. *Contracting* provides an opportunity to establish transparency about the systematic consultation process, including clarifying consultant and consultee assumptions and expectations regarding collaboration, evaluation, and confidentiality; ownership of the problem and intervention; and the consultee indicating explicit agreement to proceed with problem-solving. Even though the contracting stage is brief, it sets the tone for the consultation relationship and problem-solving process and requires nuanced application (e.g., making it a dialogue rather than a monologue). By completing the activities in this chapter, including observing and practicing contracting, we hope you begin to appreciate the complexity and centrality of this problem-solving stage.

7

PROBLEM IDENTIFICATION AND PROBLEM ANALYSIS

Look Before You Leap

> *Given an hour to solve a problem on which your life depended, I would use the first 55 minutes to ensure I was answering the right question.*
>
> *(Attributed to Einstein)*

In this chapter, we overview what we view to be the keystone stage of problem-solving: *Problem Identification and Problem Analysis (PID/PA)*. Before considering the components and processes of this stage, we would like you to explore your own assumptions and beliefs about this early stage of problem-solving.

ACTIVITY 7.1 (INDIVIDUAL)

Warm-Up Questions: PID/PA

Write down responses to the following questions. You can write sentences or just key words.

1. When you think about solving a problem, what do you view to be the most important steps?
2. How might your own assumptions and beliefs as a consultant influence how a problem is defined?
3. How might your communication skills, as discussed in prior chapters, influence how a problem is defined?
4. If a consultee wants help with more than one problem, how should problems be prioritized?
5. Defining and analyzing problems is considered a critical prerequisite to developing an intervention plan. Why do you suppose this is the case?

Given the centrality of evidence-based practices in psychology (APA, 2006) and school psychology (e.g., Kratochwill & Stoiber, 2002), we would not be surprised if your thoughts first went to consultants needing to move quickly from referral statements to identifying powerful interventions, and then to support intervention implementation. Our knowledge of and access to evidence-based academic and behavioral interventions designed for struggling students is more robust than ever before in the history of education and psychology. Indeed, we are able to identify research-based strategies with a high likelihood of success and provide these interventions to students with identified needs, such as those falling below certain curriculum-based measurement (CBM) thresholds or problematic classroom behaviors.

We agree that identifying and implementing research-based interventions is critical, and that there are often pressures, both real and imagined, to move forward quickly in problem-solving. *However, we also believe the most high-leverage stage of problem-solving is the PID/PA stage, which occurs prior to designing and implementing interventions.* The first half of the chapter offers an overview of key components and aims to provide conceptual knowledge and tools for consultants to engage successfully in *PID/PA.* Thus, the first part of the chapter focuses primarily on the *content* of *PID/PA.* The second part of the chapter offers six Big Ideas for consultants to keep in mind during this critical consultation stage, each paired with multiple examples from actual consultant-consultee interactions in schools. In essence, these Big Ideas are focused on the *process* of *PID/PA.* Activities are provided throughout the chapter for you to continue to develop your skills in identifying, operationalizing, and prioritizing problems.

The Nuts and Bolts of PID/PA

PID/PA is the second stage of problem-solving, following entry and contracting. Often *PID/PA* occurs *immediately* after the consultation is contracted, even within the same meeting, as consultees and consultants alike are eager to dive into the referral issue (being cautious here, as stated in the last chapter, not to shortcut the contracting process because of this pull into solving the referral problem). The importance of *PID/PA* cannot be overstated, because what happens within this stage determines what will be done in subsequent problem-solving stages. As has often been stated in various terms, "Problem identification is the most critical stage of consultation because it results in the design and implementation of an effective plan" (Kratochwill et al., 2014, p. 468). The purposes and components of *PID/PA* are highlighted in Table 7.1.

The culture of the school can interfere with this stage of the process. In many schools, teams and consultants operate on what Little (2007) called help and assistance. Teachers tell the helper their concern, and the team or consultant provides

TABLE 7.1 An Overview of the Problem Identification and Problem Analysis Stage of Problem-Solving

Stage	Purpose	Business to be Accomplished
Problem Identification and Problem Analysis	Create shared perception of consultee concerns Define problem in observable and measurable terms Establish baseline of current performance Establish goals	Create shared understanding of teacher's concern(s) using collaborative communication skills Define concern(s) in observable terms Follow up with additional data collection, such as record or work sample review, observation, or instructional assessment Consider student's instructional match Prioritize concerns Establish a plan to measure current performance (i.e., Baseline) Establish baseline measurement of performance Set goals based on baseline data

multiple interventions, some even evidence-based, which may or may not apply. As one consultant-in-training (CIT) explained:

> This school culture was observed within my first consultation session with the teacher. The teacher showed me this "chart intervention" that she has been using for over a month that was recommended to her at the team meeting. The student gets points deducted when he is bad and gets to keep the points and then receives a positive reinforcement at the end of the week when he is good. After viewing the chart intervention, I tried to help the teacher see how inappropriate the intervention was regarding the student's problem by asking the teacher what the student's concern is, how she is measuring the concern with this intervention, and whether it is effective. The teacher not only is frustrated and overwhelmed with the complexity of the intervention, but she states that it is not working. She cannot look at the chart intervention and tell me how any of the student's problems are recorded. As a result of the obvious ineffectiveness of the intervention, the teacher was not applying it with integrity. It was clear that the intervention did not fit the student, teacher, and classroom. More importantly, the problem was never identified or analyzed. [This is] a good example of problem-solving that does not follow best practice guidelines.

Some models of consultation imply that *PID/PA* can be completed in a single meeting or interview (e.g., Behavioral Consultation; Martens, DiGennaro Reed, & Magnusson, 2014). Our experience is that it often requires multiple consultation meetings to appropriately identify and define problems with the right data, sufficient specificity, and shared understanding to move forward to the intervention stage. Even then, consultation is often recursive, and *PID/PA* may need to be revisited if an intervention is unsuccessful, additional problems arise, or one problem is solved and then another is prioritized.

A good way to think about the kinds of problems that bring the consultee to the process was developed by Caplan (1970) in his classic text on mental health consultation. He defined four different types of problems in working with consultees:

Lack of knowledge
Lack of skill
Lack of self-confidence
Lack of professional objectivity

We have seen each of these reasons bring a consultee to ask for help. Sometimes the teacher simply lacks information. One case involved a child with seizures, and the teacher needed information about what to do if the child had a seizure in class. Many teachers need additional information on the impact of bilingualism on students' classroom performance (see Ortiz & Melo, 2017, for a good summary of what teachers should know about the impact of language issues on student outcomes). Often the consultee lacks skill, such as in classroom management strategies, or assessment of entry-level skills to determine if the student has the skill to succeed in a given lesson. In these cases, working with the teacher to develop the skills can provide a meaningful source of professional development. In cases where there is a lack of self-confidence, consultant support to the consultee can be a productive intervention. For instance, a first-year, second-grade teacher appreciated a consultant observing and affirming that students seemed very engaged during a math lesson. Finally, there are cases in which the consultee lacks objectivity, such as in the Berger (2012) case, where the teacher had developed negative assumptions about her students. Sometimes a lack of objectivity is related to issues of diversity in the classroom. We have found multiple examples where teachers perceived students of color as unable to learn. Gustafson (2012) describes her consultee teacher's initial presentation of the student as one "who could not learn" (p. 78), but through the consultation process, the child made all his goals, showing steady progress over time. Similarly, students labeled with a learning disability may also be perceived by teachers as unable to respond to the classroom activities.

Initial Problem Definition

During *PID/PA*, problems are collaboratively defined between the consultant and the consultee. Using the communication and relational skills described in previous chapters, the problem becomes *our problem* to work on *shoulder to shoulder* rather than *the consultee's problem* or a problem observed and dictated by the consultant that is not shared or owned by the consultee. Problems are defined in observable and measurable terms, including attention to *who* is the focus of the problem, *what* the problem is, *when* the problem occurs, and *where* the problem occurs.

Definitional Red Flags

Overly simplistic, high inference, or ill-defined problems will not get you and your consultee very far in problem-solving. In Chapter 4 in Table 4.1, we provided several examples of such terminology we have heard used by consultees to describe students early on in the problem identification process. Such utterances provide *red flags* alerting consultants of the need to clarify in order to assist the dyad in moving towards observable and measurable problem identification. Here is where the Ladder of Inference, also discussed in Chapter 4, becomes useful. If a consultant inadvertently affirms high inference problem definitions (e.g., "You're right, she is quite sassy," or, "It sounds like he is quite hyperactive"), the dyad risks admiring rather than solving the problem or focusing on only the student's behavior rather than any aspect of context. Alternatively, the consultant might clarify: "Tell me what you mean by sassy," or, "What does hyperactive look like in your classroom?", thereby moving down the Ladder of Inference towards observable and measurable statements of the behavior. As you develop competence in consultation, *red flags* in need of clarification will begin to stick out more clearly than might be the case as you first begin to practice consultation.

Prioritizing

Multiple concerns may surface in a flash flood of information during *PID/PA*, and you may feel drowned in details, unsure of where to direct the consultation. For example, when asked, "Can you just give me some ideas of what the problems are in the classroom that you are facing?", a teacher responded:

> Okay, um, at this point the child is functioning somewhat below grade level …. There are disciplining problems and work habit problems that we are also, um, facing right now. He has problems with self-control, with body contact and staying on-task, attending to what he's supposed to be doing, and following directions … There were language differences and different expectations … And he is also trying to make an adjustment between that, which he has been having some difficulty doing. These are some of the problems we're facing right now.

As previously described, all the key consultation communication skills, particularly active listening, clarifying, and paraphrasing, are critical during this stage. Once the dyad has discussed initial concerns with sufficient depth, it makes sense to prioritize a single problem to focus on more closely, which is exactly what the consultation dyad did in the situation described above. Prioritizing a single problem allows the dyad to hone in like a laser on the most pressing or pivotal issue rather than juggling several at once, risking all "balls" falling to the ground. Concerns that are not the first priority can be revisited later in problem-solving, or after the priority concern is mitigated (see Gifford, 2012, for an example of how this process was conducted by a CIT). Teacher consultees are often relieved to hear they can focus on one issue in a complex case, as it makes the problem they are working on more manageable and approachable. In a way, prioritizing can be viewed as an intervention in and of itself.

From a behavioral perspective, Zins and Erchul (2002) suggested that problem-solving priorities could be:

> ranked based on: (a) behaviors considered to be physically dangerous to self or others, (b) positive low frequency behaviors in need of strengthening, (c) behaviors that can be naturally reinforced in the environment, (d) behaviors viewed as essential for development, and (e) behaviors that maximize functioning in a variety of settings.
>
> *(p. 632)*

If the issue is an academic problem, attending to how well the student's entry-level skills are matched to the classroom curriculum materials (Gickling, Gravois, & Angell, 2016) is required. Even if the problem is a behavior, we believe that the academic context in which the behavior occurs always requires careful consideration. The consultant and consultee must consider whether the behavior problem is a result of a poor instructional match, in which case the problem might be resolved if instructional or task variables are adjusted in light of student variables, such as what the student knows, enabling the teacher to find the right point in the curriculum sequence for effective instruction (Gickling, Gravois, & Angell, 2016). Instructional match creates the point where both teaching and learning will be maximally successful. If a poor instructional match is indeed the issue, an instructional intervention may be an appropriate focus instead of, or in conjunction with, a behavioral intervention. Examples of instructional match variables for consideration during *PID/PA* and subsequent problem-solving stages are illustrated in Figure 7.1 (see Gickling, Gravois, & Angell, 2016, for additional information about instructional match). Barrett (2012) describes a case that shows how instructional match was helpful in producing progress for a group of students.

In sum, a variety of interrelated problems will likely arise in *PID/PA*, and it is up to you and the consultee to collaboratively determine which problem or problems to tackle first. As a dyad, you must move beyond surface-level and high-inference descriptions of problems. Examining the school context within which the difficulty is embedded is critical, whether the concern is an academic one (e.g., reading fluency, early numeracy, math calculation accuracy, completing homework, study skills) or another type of behavior (e.g., following multi-step directions, active off-task behavior, poor attendance, limited social interactions). In addition, you and the consultee will want to think about which behaviors are

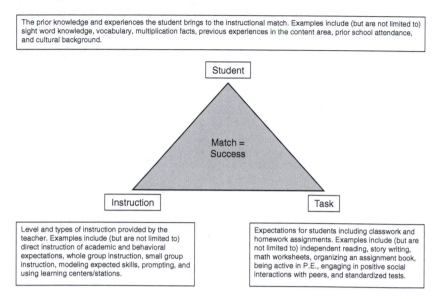

The prior knowledge and experiences the student brings to the instructional match. Examples include (but are not limited to) sight word knowledge, vocabulary, multiplication facts, previous experiences in the content area, prior school attendance, and cultural background.

Student

Match = Success

Instruction

Task

Level and types of instruction provided by the teacher. Examples include (but are not limited to) direct instruction of academic and behavioral expectations, whole group instruction, small group instruction, modeling expected skills, prompting, and using learning centers/stations.

Expectations for students including classwork and homework assignments. Examples include (but are not limited to) independent reading, story writing, math worksheets, organizing an assignment book, being active in P.E., engaging in positive social interactions with peers, and standardized tests.

FIGURE 7.1 Examples of student, instruction, and task variables in instructional match.

(a) most *salient* (e.g., consuming most of the consultee's time or attention) and (b) may be *pivotal* in their influence on other behaviors (e.g., enhancing reading skills would likely increase on-task behavior during reading activities) and therefore are likely to have the most generalizable impact for the student or students. Activity 7.2, an excerpt from an actual consultation session, provides an opportunity to help you think through early problem identification and prioritization.

ACTIVITY 7.2 (INDIVIDUAL, GROUP)

Prioritizing Problems

The following is an actual excerpt from a *PID/PA* session in which a consultant and consultee prioritized concerns to address for Libby, a first-grade student. Review the transcript and answer the subsequent questions individually and, if possible, compare responses with a partner or in a small group.

> **Consultant (C)**: Okay, so what I think I'm hearing you say is that there are four main concerns for Libby. Let's try to prioritize these four areas of concern.

> **Teacher Consultee (TC)**: I would say first the impulsivity, where she is shouting out or impulsively coming up to me without raising her hand. Second, the self-regulation. I would like to work on when it comes to structural changes and she cries because she is confused. Third, ridding her of her obsession with one peer and making more friends. Fourth, the pencil in mouth problem.

C: That sounds like a good prioritization to me.

TC: Yes, I am concerned because the impulsivity is affecting other students' work and distracting during class.

C: Yes, and as we are prioritizing these concerns, this just means we will start with the first behavior that you would like to see change in or improve on first. From there we can move to the other behaviors.

TC: Yeah, I think this would be a good place to start, because she will be able to be less egocentric and start thinking about herself and others in the classroom. Hopefully this will help with the other issues as well.

C: Yes, and it seems that you and Libby have developed a good relationship. But some of the concern is, how will Libby be in the future? It is important that Libby is equipped with strategies so that she can be self-aware and regulate her behaviors on her own. So hopefully we can think of interventions that address Libby's learning.

TC: Yes, it is very concerning about her future. I hope that I can help with teaching and learning and providing supports for Libby.

C: Well, that is very nice to hear from you. Many educators forget that they have such a large impact and the environment can play such a large role.

TC: Right, and I worry because in a few years she is going to have a more compartmentalized education. She will go to science class, social studies, math, reading… and there won't be the time to develop that sort of relationship that you can develop in primary school.

C: Yes, so I think now would be a great time to start putting in some strategies and trying some different things to help her. I think we have identified a great place to start.

Questions and Activities for Reflection:

1. Identify the four behaviors being discussed by the consultant and consultee.
   a. How well-operationalized are these behaviors?
2. How well did they determine which behaviors to prioritize?
   a. In your opinion, are the "right" behaviors prioritized? Why or why not?
   b. Should academic issues be examined? Why might you want to include those?
3. What would be your next steps as a consultant now that a behavior has been prioritized with the consultee?
   a. How would you bring these behaviors down the "Ladder of Inferences"?
   b. How might these behaviors be situated within the school-based context in which they are occurring?

Record Review, Ecological Observation, and Ecological Assessment

Imagine that you get to a point where you have talked about several problems on a surface level for about 15 minutes, and your meeting time is nearing its scheduled end. Again, you might perceive pressure to offer solutions (i.e., interventions) although the problem that needs to be addressed remains murky. At this point it is a common experience for CITs to feel *stuck*, unsure how to proceed. We propose that you and your consultee discuss what additional information is needed and decide on strategies, such as reviewing student records, observing the instructional environment, and/or conducting an instructional assessment.

Reviewing records, work samples, and curriculum materials. You may dive into a consultation with limited knowledge or information about a student. It makes sense to gather more information before the consultation begins and/or immediately after a first meeting when you have a better idea of the consultee's concern. One source of helpful information will be relevant work samples. For example, if an initial concern expressed by a consultee is that a third-grade student is "struggling with math," it would be helpful to learn more about the scope and sequence of the curriculum, classroom instruction, and how the teacher assesses student mastery. Following that, you may wish to look at in-class assignments, the student's patterns of performance (e.g., error analysis), and, if possible, normative comparisons with peers.

More global records may also be helpful, such as looking at the student's prior school history, including attendance, report cards, performance on state tests, and school-level benchmarking data such as CBMs. For example, if a student is already in a remedial reading program, based on a screening test at Tier 1, but not making progress, the particular reading program in which she is placed may not be appropriate; the screening test may not have identified her specific concern, and additional instructional assessment information may be required before the lack of progress triggers a special education referral. In fact, using screening data without additional instructional assessment of a student's knowns and unknowns within the curriculum can lead to poor decisions about intervention that delay the student's progress. In addition, some data may be misleading. For example, just because a student is performing well on standardized or norm-referenced assessments, it does not guarantee they are well-matched instructionally within the classroom (Gickling et al., 2016). Therefore, a record review, but in conjunction with information related to the classroom and provided by the teacher, may be appropriate.

Ecological observation. In addition to reviewing records and permanent products such as work samples, you may wish to observe in relevant settings during the times in which the problems are occurring. Observations should focus not only on the student or students of concern but the larger instructional context. Imagine attending a baseball game and only focusing your observations on first base. While you would observe the ball come and go occasionally, you would miss the rest of the action on the field. Similarly, it is beneficial to consider how the student is situated within the classroom or other setting (e.g., lunchroom, transitions, recess) rather than just observing the student.

It is beyond the scope of this chapter and book to go into depth regarding observational techniques and foci. Ysseldyke and Christenson's (2002) functional assessment of academic behavior (FAAB) provides several areas for consideration in observing instruction. These include:

- Instructional match (material is not too easy and not too difficult for the student(s) referred);
- Instructional expectations (high but realistic for amount and accuracy, and clearly communicated);
- Classroom environment (positive, supportive classroom management);
- Instructional presentation (clearly presented; sufficient information in directions; teacher checks for understanding);
- Motivational strategies (techniques are included to enhance student interest);
- Relevant practice (several opportunities for accurate practice);
- Informed feedback (immediate, specific feedback, including corrections as needed);
- Academic engaged time (active engagement/responsiveness to content);
- Adaptive instruction (curriculum is reasonably adjusted/differentiated to meet individual students' needs);
- Progress evaluation (direct, frequent, formative assessment of student progress, which informs future instruction); and
- Student understanding (accurate understanding of what to do and how to do it).

In addition to the FAAB, a number of other observational techniques may be relevant, such as the classroom checkup (Reinke, Lewis-Palmer, & Merrell, 2008), and the behavioral observation of students in schools (Pearson, 2013). Regardless of which tool is used, we believe problems are best understood within an ecological context, including a consideration of instructional context.

Observation discussions can focus on the student as situated within the classroom context. Care needs to be taken in communicating observational data to the consultee during this stage for the results to be well-received. Clear agreement on the focus in advance of the observation is essential, although sometimes the observation uncovers some unexpected findings. It is always useful to provide the raw data so that the analysis can be conducted together with the teacher; this is even more essential if the data have some unexpected surprises for the teacher. For example, in one case, a CIT's observation in a kindergarten classroom during center time (where students worked independently at activity areas set up around the classroom) clearly indicated that many students were engaging in inappropriate behavior and that both the quality of the activities and classroom management of the centers were inadequate. The teacher had brought up one student in the consultation, but it was clear from the observation that the problem behavior was widely shared. The shared discussion of the observation data guided the teacher toward considering broad-based classroom management strategies rather than a single, intensive behavior intervention for one child. The communication skills of clarifying and perception checking became useful adjuncts to this consultation session as the implications of the observation became apparent to the teacher.

Ecological academic assessment. A third way additional data may be gathered is through processes of academic assessment to determine instructional match. In fact, the Instructional Consultation (IC) model requires an ecological academic assessment in almost every case of a classroom concern. Consultants without a strong background in academic assessment and instruction often focus on classroom behavior rather than a connection between behavior and academic frustration of students.

Ecological academic assessment strategies include instructional assessment (Gickling et al., 2016) or curriculum-based assessment by instructional design (Burns & Parker, 2014). Although a full review of these techniques is beyond the scope of the chapter and book, readers are referred to these resources for details on working with consultees to implement ecological academic assessment practices. The idea is that we can assess students within an ecological academic framework that accounts for students' prior knowledge and experiences, task expectations, and instructional practices with a focus on these questions (Gickling et al., 2016):

> What does the student know?
> What can the student do?
> How does the student think?
> How does the student approach unfamiliar tasks?
> What can the teacher do?

These questions are helpful conceptualizers during *PID/PA*, as well as throughout the entirety of the problem-solving process.

Baseline

After a concern is prioritized, whether an academic or behavior issue, and some additional information is gathered through records, observation, or ecological instructional assessment strategies, you and the consultee will continue to work to achieve an observable and measurable definition of the problem (including who, what, where, and when). When it is clear that the problem is operationally defined, the identified problem can be measured precisely and becomes the statement of current performance, or baseline. Once the baseline is measured, this level of performance can be used to set goals for improvement. During the intervention evaluation stage of problem-solving, goals can be considered in conjunction with this baseline to determine if the intervention is working, and if not, what can be done about it.

Goal-Setting

Goals stem directly from the baseline data; they specify an aim line for closing gaps between a student's current performance and expected performance in the problem area that you have prioritized. Goal statements focus on alterable, measurable behaviors; set benchmarks for a standard of comparison; specify target dates for completion; and set standards or social comparisons to consider progress (Kratochwill et al., 2014). Whenever possible, desirable performance should be the focus of a goal, even when the problem is maladaptive behavior (Pluymert, 2014). For example, in one consultation case (Pas, 2012), a CIT and consultee agreed to focus on *increasing* a target student's verbal requests to peers as a replacement behavior for invading of peers' space, and set goals on the former behavior rather than the latter.

Knowledge of the scope and sequence of the curriculum is essential to academic goal-setting as it indicates formative and summative expectations for student progress in that grade level and classroom. It is also essential to know the teacher's expectations for students, both academically and behaviorally, as there is sometimes misalignment with the curriculum. One teacher expected all kindergarten students in her high-achieving school to be able read upon entering school, and indeed, many did; however, it was beyond the curricular expectations for kindergarten. It is not difficult to imagine the challenges a non-reader would have in this class despite not technically beginning the year below grade level.

Goal-Setting Methods

Several approaches can be used for goal-setting. For now, let us consider three approaches that CITs in our classes have found helpful in their cases: the use of norms, splitting the difference, and the 25% rule. Irrespective of which of these approaches (or if another approach) is used, remember that goals should be established collaboratively with the consultee, consistent with the entire collaborative problem-solving process.

Normative data provide consultants and consultees information regarding typical rates of students' academic or behavior progress and expected levels of performance. National norms, such as those established by curriculum-based measures, are appropriate to use when these data are aligned with the target behavior (e.g., reading fluency) and the local curriculum's scope and sequence (e.g., sometimes the order of curricular objectives can differ between reading programs). However, local norms (e.g., classroom, school, district) have the advantage of providing estimates of typical performance specific to your setting, curriculum, or a particular population (e.g., ELL students in your school). For example, in one case a teacher consultee collected weekly brief written responses from all students in her class. When one student was struggling with writing, the teacher worked with a CIT to analyze writing samples according to a scoring rubric (Tindal & Hasbrouck, 1991). The permanent product data acted as both a baseline measure and a way to assess student progress over multiple weeks for all students in her class. Typical rates of progress could be used to estimate short-term (e.g., 4 to 6 weeks) and long-term (e.g., 12 weeks) goals for the student. The use of local norms also allows the consultant and consultee to consider if other students they had not initially targeted would also benefit from an intervention.

Another way to set goals is the split the difference method. The dyad begins by estimating short-term and long-term goals, which are informed by available information such as norms, the curriculum, or teacher expectations. The short-term goal can then be subtracted from the long-term goal, and the difference between them divided in half to estimate an interim goal. Once the intervention is implemented, the dyad will determine the ongoing rate of progress made by the student and readjust the interim goal as needed.

The 25% rule posits that for many problems, a short-term improvement of 25% would demonstrate strong initial progress. Therefore, after measuring baseline data, the dyad takes 25% of the baseline and adds that number to the baseline to create a short-term goal. For example, if a student is reading 30 words per minute, $30 \times .25$ is 7.5, and therefore the short-term goal would be 37.5 words per minute in approximately six weeks. Given the student's progress over those first few weeks, the consultant and teacher can estimate a rate of improvement. Again, the long-term goal is established based on where the dyad ultimately would like to see the student perform. While it is easy to calculate the short-term goal using the 25% method, it is possible to over- or underestimate the short-term goal.

Documenting PID/PA

One tool that has been developed to document the problem-solving process, including *PID/PA* and subsequent stages, is the Student Documentation Form (SDF; see Appendix D). Although the tool was developed specifically for the implementation of IC (Gravois, Gickling, & Rosenfield, 2011; Rosenfield, 2012), we find its features are relevant to any model of consultation, including the SC model presented in this book. Although additional training on the SDF would be helpful, at a minimum, a consultant can use this tool to write out and prioritize problems with the consultee, as well as document the intervention upon which the consultation dyad has agreed. The use of the graph is a tool to help monitor progress and is linked with enhanced problem-solving outcomes for students (Fuchs & Fuchs, 1986). The school in which you are doing your consulting work might have its own tool or process to document problem-solving. Regardless of which tool you use, it should (a) clearly document and guide the entire problem-solving process, including the identified concern with baseline data, description of the intervention, and the implementation schedule (who, what, when, where); (b) include a graph documenting student progress; and (c) be used in a collaborative manner with your consultee.

PID/PA Big Ideas

Up to now we have focused on describing the nuts and bolts of the *PID/PA* stage, or the *content* of *PID/PA*. Next we turn to six Big Ideas, summarized in Table 7.2. We urge you to keep these Big Ideas in mind as you engage in the *PID/PA* stage, as they should inform the *process* of interactions during this stage. Further, since the consultation process is recursive, and each problem-solving

TABLE 7.2 Big Ideas Informing Problem Identification in School-Based Consultation Problem-Solving

Big Ideas Informing Problem Identification
1. Complex problems, such as those found in schools, rarely have simple or linear solutions;
2. The problems school consultants attempt to solve are situated within a school-based context, and should be defined accordingly;
3. Everything we do is an intervention, beginning from the earliest consultation interactions and including the establishment of a shared problem conceptualization occurring during PID;
4. Problem operationalization stems from listening and seeking clarification, not from asking scripted questions, and communication skills are critical;
5. Accurate problem operationalization precedes well-matched intervention planning;
6. More data aren't necessarily better data when it comes to understanding and solving problems.

stage is interdependent on the others, these Big Ideas are relevant through the entirety of consultation.

Big Idea #1: Complex problems, such as those found in schools, rarely have simple or linear solutions. Consultees often request consultation in search of a "magic wand" or a "silver bullet" to make the problem they are facing instantly disappear. This is not surprising in school settings given the tremendous demands associated with classroom instruction and management. Simultaneously, CITs are eager to learn as many interventions as possible, hoping to fill up their toolboxes with "silver bullet solutions" to prescribe to teachers requesting assistance. Although occasionally a simple problem and solution do occur, it is not the norm. Consistent with Schein's (2013, 2016) work on process consultation and humble consulting, there are a number of flawed assumptions with a failure to recognize this complexity.

First, there are instances where consultees may know that something is not working in the classroom but not know why it is not working, perhaps because the correct problem has not yet been identified. Imagine a consultee describing an impression of the problem (e.g., "Dave is not putting forth effort") and a consultant prescribing an intervention from this initial description (e.g., a motivating sticker chart with opportunities for Dave to earn stickers). However, what if the problem is actually that Dave is frustrated or bored with the material? Thus, the intervention may not be well-matched to address the root of the problem.

Second, sometimes consultees are looking for the consultant to diagnose the problem and offer a solution. This presumes (a) an accurate diagnosis from the consultant, who may not be familiar with the problem; (b) that the consultee will accept the diagnosis; and (c) that the consultee will accept, implement, and adhere to prescribed solutions. A breakdown at any of these steps is possible. The consultant's diagnosis may be incorrect, as in the previous example. Even if it is correct, the consultee may not agree with the diagnosis or may not want to or be able to implement the solution—even if it is an excellent, evidence-based intervention. Schein (2013, 2016) suggests that collaborative assessment and intervention design will support a collaborative problem-solving process that promotes professional learning for the consultee. Activity 7.3 contains a transcribed excerpt from a *PID/PA* session and demonstrates Big Idea #1. Read through the transcript and consider the subsequent questions.

ACTIVITY 7.3 (INDIVIDUAL, GROUP)

Big Idea #1

The following is an actual excerpt from a *PID/PA* session in which a consultant and consultee were identifying concerns for several first-grade students, beginning with Kyle. Review the transcript and answer the subsequent questions individually and, if possible, compare responses with a partner or in a small group.

> **Teacher Consultee (TC)**: Okay. When are we going to start something in the class and get something going, because I really need it.

> **Consultant (C)**: Well, that's part of what the [Evidence-Based Intervention] is about, which is why I think it's important to go through, because it's basically going through…

> **TC**: Is there any way that you could maybe do a small group, too? Like sooner, so we can start them on trying to do something?

> **C**: Yeah, about? So, you are not clear what this group is intervening about, are you?

> **TC**: You know, shouting out even, that would be fine. Being disrespectful. Kyle's very disrespectful, to me, to his classmates, to whoever the teacher is.

> **C**: That's obviously an issue.

> **TC**: And the opposite is another student, Deanna: she sucks her thumb and hides in her shirt, doesn't look at you … walks away, doesn't answer. So maybe even if you put them together [in an intervention group], they're together on other things. If you put them together, they could learn how to get in the middle … And then I have this other one, Marjorie … She's okay, she's pretty quiet, and she could probably benefit from it too.

> **C**: A small group is definitely something we can get going separately, I just really wanted to have something in place in your classroom that we can collaborate on.

> **TC**: Yeah, I just wanted to … That's fine too, but I need Kyle to get started on something, because Check In Check Out does nothing.

C: And that's something, too ... looking at the match between the student, the instruction, and the task so when you set up the student for success in the classroom it really...

TC: I mean, he needs instant praise 24 hours a day. I always have feathers; I try to give him feathers. I try to call on him, but I can't call on him every single time. I try to call on him, and then I call on someone else two seconds later, and he gets upset. Because he is the world. And I can't ... because then if you call on him all the time, then Deanna starts crying, and then she doesn't get a feather, and then multiple other things happen...

C: And that's something that we can really work on too. It seems contradictory, because when you have students displaying these problem behaviors, what [the Evidence-Based Intervention] suggests is that you promote frequent positive interactions with them. They need more. An average student maybe needs a "great, good job," but the students who misbehave so much need that ratio to increase. Which is kind of counterintuitive.

TC: So if there's any way you can do anything with those three [students]... Or maybe you can even do something with Kyle.

Questions for Reflection:

This is not a simple issue to address, is it! But let's begin with the most basic issue, operationally defining a complex situation.

1. What problem or problems(s) are the consultant and consultee working on?
   a. In your opinion, are the problems sufficiently defined? Why or why not?
   b. How would you move forward to define behaviors?
2. The consultant has an evidence-based intervention in mind. Identify some problems with offering this intervention at this point in the process.

Big Idea #2: The problems school consultants attempt to solve are situated within a school-based context and should be defined accordingly. When defining problems, consultants and consultees sometimes get distracted with *red herrings*, issues that are peripheral to the problem-solving task. Red herrings include storytelling about students or students' familial contexts and labeling within-child pathology without connecting to concrete behaviors on which to focus intervention within the classroom. This is also sometimes referred to as *admiring the problem*. Knotek (2003), for example, described the irrelevant talk about the homes of students in his qualitative study of problem-solving consultation teams. Similarly, Sherry (2012) found in her school "a lot of storytelling at the meetings ... there was talk about students' family homes and behaviors unrelated to the concern on the agenda" (p. 100).

Problems should be defined with reference to the school-based context in which they are situated so that consultants and consultees avoid lingering on red herrings. For example, it may be helpful for a consultant to bond (recall the *bond and move strategy* in Chapter 4) with a teacher who expresses frustration about a student, but dwelling on this information may actually be detrimental to moving forward in problem-solving. Instead, focusing on what we can do to support the student within the classroom context should be of primary concern. Consider how you might respond to the teacher or social worker in the next activity if you were the consultant.

ACTIVITY 7.4 (INDIVIDUAL, GROUP)

Problem-Solving Within Ecological Context

Look at the following actual interaction between a teacher consultee and social worker consultee about an academic problem during a consultation about a first-grade student. Answer the subsequent questions individually and, if possible, compare responses with a partner or in a small group.

> **Teacher Consultee**: I still don't think we really understand what the problem is up here (points to head). There is something wrong.

> **Social Worker Consultee**: And we are not neurologists.

Questions for Reflection:

1. If you were the consultant, how would you respond to these comments?

As described earlier in this chapter, and in Chapter 1, consulting ecologically or with an ecobehavioral lens means thinking about the student and his or her interactions with the curriculum, the teacher's instruction and management strategies, and the broader school culture. When problems are operationalized with instructional factors in mind, problems become *solvable* within the classroom setting. Behavioral problems are also initially situated within an instructional context, as misbehavior may result from things like unclear instructional expectations, insufficient motivational techniques, or instructional match that is too easy or frustrating for the student. And, some behaviors result from inadequate classroom management strategies.

The following transcribed excerpt demonstrates how a CIT worked with a second-grade teacher consultee to move from storytelling to a more focused, school-situated problem definition over the course of one *PID/PA* session. We have included *italicized written reflection* by the consultant regarding the transcription, which demonstrates her struggle to help move the dyad towards a focus within the consultee's classroom setting in which they could realistically intervene.

CIT: In addition to the Reading Mastery [pullout intervention], what kind of support would you expect her to get [in your classroom]?

Teacher Consultee (TC): I almost feel like maybe we need to have some kind of meeting with mom, the nurse, and me. And say, "these are the expectations. She needs her medicine." I wonder if either the medicine is not right or she is not getting it. Because her being out of her seat… something is wrong with that. And then from there, maybe seeing how that goes if her medicine is changed. Because I know the Reading Mastery teacher is seeing the same behaviors where she is totally not focused, she is worried about "what's in your lunch"; I guess is something she says a lot, because the other teacher's lunch is on her desk … she is unfocused.

CIT: So how could that meeting happen? Could you arrange it? Who needs to arrange it?

TC: Well, the problem is that mom doesn't have a working phone…

CIT: So getting ahold of her is a problem.

TC: Yeah.

CIT: So does a letter need to be sent home? Have you been able to communicate with her that way?

TC: Yeah, and she expects that packet to be filled out, and I've started but that's a process in itself; it is like 11 pages…

CIT: So maybe that is an opportunity where she could get the packet, and you could also meet…

TC: Well, the packet has to be mailed to the Social Security office.

The teacher continued to express obstacles to meeting with [the student's] mom. I think this piece of our conversation is an example of our different agendas in the conversation. I was "solution-focused," while the teacher was interested in venting. It got us into a back-and-forth without ever reaching a solution. The discussion led back to the student and special education, so I tried to rephrase the original question:

CIT: What would those minutes be? What would that support look like?

TC: First of all, she would have to be tested. So I guess that would be the start to see how low she really is, and then from there I could say, "well, she should get support in this and this…" definitely math. Well, definitely reading, but I would think math too.

CIT: Okay, so she is getting reading support, and you would think that she would need additional to that, and also some support in math?

TC: Yeah. Here is her report card.

Again, I felt that the conversation veered off from my goal. So, I tried to restate my question a third time:

> **CIT:** What additional support would you want her to get in addition to Reading Mastery?
>
> **TC:** Sight words … blending. I know Reading Mastery is blending, but I think she needs more of it, consistently.
>
> **CIT:** So I'm just thinking, if we could take what is already going on in Reading Mastery. So, if we are focusing on one thing at a time, which would be that reading is your biggest concern, she is getting Reading Mastery; she does probably need a little more time to see progress. What could we do in the classroom to reinforce what she is doing with Reading Mastery? Like sounds and blending. Maybe she is not getting that sight word component and she needs that also.

Following this interchange, the dyad went on to more clearly define the student's current reading skills and needs and eventually planned an intervention focused on streamlining and supplementing the supports she was already receiving. Notably, over multiple subsequent sessions, the conversation did not return to a focus on medication or familial context, two issues that were outside of the dyad's immediate control.

Big Idea #3: Everything we do is an intervention. When we discuss interventions, we tend to think of large Evidence-Based Interventions (EBIs) such as universal, targeted, or intensive reading or behavior programs, or intervention components such as increasing praise for appropriate behavior, providing additional opportunities for accurate practice, or clarifying task expectations. However, as argued by Schein (1999), everything we do as consultants can be considered an intervention, beginning with our earliest interactions with consultees. We call these small interactions with the potential to make large impacts *process interventions (ProInts)*. One example of a *ProInt* is clarifying the consultation process up front during the *Contracting* stage of problem-solving; this helps you and the consultee get on the same page for how you will approach the problem-solving process and what it will mean to work collaboratively. Another example of a *ProInt* is demonstrating support for the consultee by listening and perspective taking, rather than moving forward with your own agenda without acknowledging the consultee's concerns.

ProInts stimulate ripples in the problem-solving pond. For example, how consultees think about (representation) and talk about (presentation) problems may shift as a result of *ProInts*, which in turn alters the way an intervention will be designed, implemented, and evaluated in subsequent problem-solving stages. Hylander (2017) describes the process of a *turning* in her work in Sweden, the idea that how a problem is conceptualized and presented needs to change through the consultation process into a concern that can be resolved.

Following is an example of a consultee's changing frame of a problem, again from a real example as described by the consultant in a final reflection, demonstrating a turning in one teacher's problem representation and presentation:

After 18 weeks of working together, the teacher was still open to share what she's been working on with the student and how things are going. On my part, I think I offered a lot of support through listening, sharing my representation of the problem, and simply keeping the process going. A couple of weeks after being asked to reflect on what would change when her student would meet eligibility criteria for special education, the teacher told me that she knew that special education eligibility won't change the fact that Amalia would still be her student, and the teacher would be looking for ways to include her in the general curriculum because she felt confident in that and in knowing what Amalia can do. For me, this was the greatest metamorphosis and turning in my teacher's perception about the student that began from the "student can't do" attitude to being empowered to do more things with the student on her instructional level. This turning had an impact on how the teacher was engaged in implementing our interventions.

You can further reflect on the process of conceptual turnings by completing Activity 7.5.

ACTIVITY 7.5 (INDIVIDUAL, GROUP)

Big Idea #3

The following are actual excerpts from a teacher consultee over the course of multiple *PID/PA* sessions in which a consultant and consultee were identifying concerns for a first-grade student, Amalia. Review the examples and answer the subsequent questions individually and, if possible, compare responses with a partner or in a small group.

Initial Presentation Statements	Subsequent Presentation Statements
• She has forgotten how to act in school—not that she was doing great with that—but she was catching on to a few things, and I moved a few desks because they were all irritated with each other.	• And there are workbook pages that go with that, too, that have the same characters in it, and we'll have the same sounds, so I'll be working on that. She did more when we were doing worksheets, so when there is one word that starts with the letter *B*, she can usually find it, but if there are two that start with the letter *B*, we have to start looking at. Maybe I can look at the end of the word, because yesterday we had *boot* and *book*, and she wasn't sure

- Yes, it is a new group and some-body she gets along with, but she cannot sit down, she can't pay attention, she's talking all the time.
- I'm not sure if here is the best placement. I don't make those decisions and I understand the least restrictive [environment], but I also look at her come and go, and she needs a lot of attention. There is no classroom teacher with 26 kids who has time to do that. If there were two teachers and 20 kids, maybe.

which one was which, so she is still looking at the beginning of the word. It's a huge improve-ment from where she was.
- There is a lot of improvement and a lot of things to do. She is a little more independent in a sense … she says "I can do that" or … even when we started telling time and she wasn't sure about how to do. But we've only done a little bit, and once I showed her how to do it, it was like, okay!

Questions for Reflection:

1. What differences do you notice between the earlier *PID/PA* sessions and the later *PID/PA* sessions in terms of how the teacher consultee repre-sents the problem?
2. What are the implications for the differences for problem solvability?
3. What process interventions (ProInts) can you think of that might have shifted the course of problem-solving, including a teacher's representa-tion and presentation of a student problem, in the ways demonstrated by this example?

Big Idea #4: Problem operationalization stems from listening and seek-ing clarification, not from asking scripted questions; communication skills are critical. During all problem stages, especially the *PID/PA* stage, the most foundational communication skills you can apply are paraphrasing and clari-fying the information offered by the consultee. As you listen carefully to the con-sultee's presentation of the problem, you can begin to see the problem through the consultee's eyes.

Listening can be difficult, especially for CITs. Bringing a script of pre-packaged questions to the consultation session without knowing what information the con-sultee is going to offer can make it even more difficult for you to be mindful or fully present in a consultation meeting. It is easy to become too focused on what to ask or say next rather than what the consultee is saying. In turn, you may not accurately hear the consultee's concerns or, worse yet, respond in a manner that is far removed from how the consultee is conceptualizing the problem. Such interac-tions can be detrimental to (a) building a relationship based on genuine interest in the consultee's problem and (b) co-conceptualizing the right problem to solve.

This is not to suggest that you should arrive to the consultation session unprepared. In advance of a meeting, you can take actions such as gathering appropriate background case information and think through pertinent points for clarification and discussion. However, such an agenda should be flexible and adapted based on the emergent needs of the consultee and the student or students of concern.

Following is an example of a consultation with an art teacher consultee. After the teacher shared some information, the CIT asked a scripted question without clearly having listened to the teacher:

> **Teacher Consultee (TC)**: They have a lot of free time in here, and it really backfires on us. It's the constant noise level. They do get out of their seats a lot, they make excuses to sharpen their pencils, and they get up to use the hand sanitizer 300 times a day. So, they want to do everything opposite of what I'm telling them to do.
>
> **CIT**: Do you notice a time of day when … is this happening at the beginning of the period with them?

Although it is appropriate for the CIT to be thinking about what time of day the behavior was occurring, the question was poorly phrased and did not stem directly from information provided by the teacher. Instead, the CIT might have used a clarifying statement such as: "Tell me more about the free time," or paraphrased and clarified: "It sounds like you have expectations that are not being followed. What are some of those expectations?" Arguably, such communications would have been more successful in demonstrating that the CIT was listening and then moving to clarify the consultee's information, which was too broad to specify patterns (e.g., "300 times a day").

Given the CIT's question, here was the consultee's response:

> **TC**: It's the whole hour. Sometimes they walk in noisy, and I have to get them to line up in the hallway. I say, "Okay, guys, when I have to start the day like this …" I try to be really calm. Sometimes they walk in and they're so loud it's ridiculous. It's tricky, because when we start off the day on the wrong foot … and there is a good group of kids—they're amazing. And, they are irritated because we're starting 5 minutes later. They yell at each other, like, "Stop talking! We're going to get in trouble!" You hear a lot of that, and you feel bad, because…

Although more information was offered, it didn't get the dyad much further in terms of operationalizing the problem.

Next, the CIT took a more flexible approach in her communication, offering information that she had noticed in a recent classroom observation, which was related to what she heard the teacher describe. The observation description affirmed some of the teacher's positive instructional practices. This interaction moved them forward in problem-solving more effectively and led to more specific behavioral description. Activity 7.6 is a good opportunity to practice the communication skills presented in Chapter 4.

ACTIVITY 7.6 (INDIVIDUAL, GROUP)

Big Idea #4

Read the following excerpt from an actual consultation session. Based on the underlined pieces of information from the teacher consultee (TC) in this transcript, answer the subsequent questions individually and, if possible, compare responses with a partner or in a small group.

> **CIT**: When I was here [observing], I felt like they did a really good job with putting effort into their masks and following the directions you were giving. You're always doing hands-on activities.
>
> **TC**: I haven't thought about that, really. I'll have to pay closer attention to that. They'll go in waves. If they're engaged in their activity, the noise level sometimes does get louder. Then I'll break and say, 'freeze', and sometimes it works. Sometimes I'll turn off the lights, or I'll redirect them to the carpet. It's okay to talk ... you'll have the kids that are talking but are doing what they're supposed to be doing shouting at the kids that aren't, and it'll take more minutes out of art. My guess is that when they're more involved in the activity, [they'll get louder].

Questions and Activities for Reflection:

1. How would you respond to demonstrate you heard the teacher? Write a response and identify the communication skill(s) you are using.
2. How would you respond to continue to move forward in identifying observable and measurable problems? Write a response and identify the communication skill(s) you are using.

Big Idea #5: Accurate problem operationalization precedes well-matched intervention planning. Before selecting and then implementing an intervention, it is necessary to first clearly operationalize the problem. This is a consistent theme throughout the text and is logical considering *PID/PA* precedes intervention. However, consultants still often fall into the trap of offering solutions prior to the dyad adequately understanding the problem. Activity 7.7 compares two transcriptions in two different consultation cases. Review the transcriptions and answer the questions.

ACTIVITY 7.7 (INDIVIDUAL, GROUP)

Big Idea #5

Read the following excerpts from actual consultation meetings. Answer the subsequent questions individually and, if possible, compare responses with a partner or in a small group.

Actual consultation excerpt from a meeting between a consultant and a kindergarten teacher for a student named Charlie	Actual consultation excerpt from a meeting between a consultant and a kindergarten teacher for a student named Javier
Consultant (C): So last week when we met, we started talking about how Charlie is impulsive in class and he does things like not raising his hand and shouting out. Could you give me more examples of that impulsivity in the classroom?	**Teacher Consultee (TC)**: I would say defiance. Like defiance if you ask him to do something, he will look at you and walk away. Or he will escape and find something else that he ... he'll go and talk to a different teacher. We have two teachers in here. So he'll go and try and talk to me. If I give him a prompt to go do something, he'll go and talk to the other teacher, and he's constantly just avoiding doing tasks.
Teacher Consultee (TC): He doesn't sit still very well on the carpet, and I don't know if that's because he's bigger and he's not comfortable ... his legs are always out and he's hitting people. He tries, you know, and he's always apologizing, but I don't think he's aware he's moving so much until a kid looks at him like, "you just bumped me!" So that whole ... "this is my space and I should stay in it" isn't always working for him...	**Consultant (C)**: So it seems that Javier has trouble following through with instructions and he is avoiding it by either going and talking to other students or teachers. Is that distracting in the classroom to other students?
C: Tell me a little more about the carpet and how that works with the kids.	**TC**: Yes. Especially when we're on the carpet and we're all so close together and he'll constantly try to talk to other kids or turn his body around or laugh or make jokes. And that gets the rest of the kids around him off-task.
TC: They each have a square that they sit in, so sometimes I have noticed that he does have a hard time because the squares ... I mean, they're not little, but...	
C: And he's not exactly a little kid...	

TC: He takes up the whole square because he's not a little kid ... so there have been times when I've moved him: "ok, you can sit in this square because there's no one in front of you, and then if you have to put your feet out you can put your feet out ... but you can't do that if you want to sit in the middle of the carpet because that's someone else's space in front of you." Sometimes he doesn't like to move away from the class and he tries, you can see he's thinking, "sit still, sit still," but then he might not always be paying attention as much to what we are doing...

C: So I guess next time we could discuss possible interventions for that. Is that something that sounds good to you?

TC: Yes, I would love to have something to implement in the classroom to help him.

Questions and Activities for Reflection:

1. For each column, write down an observable and measurable problem with the information that you have.
2. Of these two excerpts, which one do you believe demonstrates a more clearly-defined problem?
3. Of these two excerpts, which would be easier to intervene upon at this point in time?
4. For the less well-defined problem, what information would you need to get closer to a clearly operationalized problem?

The dialogue on the left shows how in a brief interaction, a dyad may move from a problem definition that is high on the Ladder of Inferences and internal to a child ("impulsivity") to a more clearly defined problem, in this case, Charlie's carpet square being too small for his body. We can surmise that the carpet setup was an antecedent to the student's behavior, whether the behavior was defined as impulsive, off-task, disrespectful, disruptive, or anything else. Indeed, once an intervention was implemented to adjust Charlie's carpet square, he experienced dramatic behavioral improvement. Meanwhile, the dyad on the right side of the column had more difficulty determining appropriate next steps for an intervention because the problem was not yet well-defined.

Big Idea #6: More data aren't necessarily better data when it comes to understanding and solving problems. Consultative problem-solving is akin to solving a mystery, with the consultant in the role of detective. Therefore, let's take some advice from the great Sherlock Holmes about solving problems:

"The principle difficulty in your case," remarked Holmes in his didactic fashion, "lay in the fact of there being too much evidence. What was vital was overlaid and hidden by what was irrelevant. Of all the facts which were presented to us we had to pick just those which we deemed to be essential, and then piece them together in their order, so as to reconstruct this very remarkable chain of events."

(Conan Doyle, 1894, p. 236)

Indeed, consultants and consultees are often awash with data, some of which is vital to the case and some of which is irrelevant or distracting. For example, one consultation dyad was unsure how to proceed when a fifth grader's nationally-normed CBM data indicated reading fluency to be comparable with peers, but the student struggled to read fluently in the classroom setting. Although both pieces of data were relevant to understanding the problem, the CIT needed to refocus the consultation to the student's and teacher's experience of the problem in the classroom setting and the context of a high-achieving school culture. In another instance, a teacher consultee frequently referenced data from a student's special education evaluation, including cognitive assessment scores, in trying to define the problem. The frustrated CIT did not believe these data were relevant to their problem identification or intervention planning but was unsure how to redirect the consultation focus.

Activity 7.8 demonstrates how a CIT effectively used data within a *PID/PA* session to move problem-solving forward. Review this activity and answer the subsequent questions.

ACTIVITY 7.8 (INDIVIDUAL, GROUP)

Big Idea #6, Part I

The following is an actual excerpt from a *PID/PA* session in which a consultant and consultee prioritized concerns to address for a third-grade student named Logan. Review the transcript and answer the subsequent questions individually and, if possible, compare responses with a partner or in a small group.

Consultant (C): Yeah, and I noticed a pattern at the end of each of the independent tasks. If it was something he finished before everyone else, that's when he'd start being, I guess not off-task because he was done with the task, but it was disruptive, like movement or noise, something like that. That can be something we could focus on.

Teacher Consultee (TC): Great.

C: Then these tasks that he didn't finish early, like he was working until the end, then he didn't do that.

TC: Right. That's great. I'm glad that you were able, because now it makes sense looking at the data. But like, in my head I would never have been able to process that at the end of each independent session.

[later in the same session]

TC: Yeah, it was a review sheet, which actually makes sense, because he would have already known it.

C: Okay, so review sheet, and he was extra noisy. So maybe on days like that when he doesn't need the review as much as other students ... and then January 8 ...

TC: January 8 was the beginning of the unit, so we really hadn't done much of it. It's higher-order numbers, writing numbers into the millions, which is pretty challenging for kids because they can't read it.

C: And he wasn't very disruptive. Aha!!!

TC: And also, it might be interesting, we're doing another review sheet next week. It might be interesting to calculate the review sheet day again just to see if it's consistent. All right, great, thank you, that's exciting to see a pattern; that's kind of cool!

Questions and Activities for Reflection:

1. How did data help the dyad identify a pattern that was important for identifying the "right" problem to work on?
2. How might other data have been misleading?

Activity 7.9 is intended to help CITs think through the common challenge of discussing data with a consultee when the data differ from the consultee's description of the problem.

ACTIVITY 7.9 (INDIVIDUAL, GROUP)

Big Idea #6, Part II

Sometimes it can be difficult to share observation data with a consultee, particularly if what you observe is different than what the consultee reports is happening. Read the following case study and then answer the subsequent questions individually and, if possible, compare responses with a partner or in a small group.

As part of a consultation case, you observe in the classroom to support a student named Lucinda, who the teacher reports is having behavioral difficulties. You observe a chaotic classroom lacking one or more of the features from Ysseldyke and Christenson's FAAB, as described earlier in this chapter. Lucinda is no more "off-task" than others in the class.

Questions and Activities for Reflection:

1. How might you approach this conversation with the teacher consultee?
2. What challenges do you predict might arise in this conversation?

Summary

PID/PA is considered the most pivotal stage in the SC model, an essential prerequisite to successful intervention. During *PID/PA*, the consultant and consultee create a shared understanding of problem(s) to be solved through discussion, observation, and data collection; they prioritize a concern to be addressed first; define the problem in observable and measurable terms; measure baseline performance; and establish goals to close the gap between current performance and expected performance. Since consultation is an indirect service, consultants attend to consultee needs (i.e., knowledge, skill, self-confidence, and professional objectivity), in addition to student needs during this stage.

There are numerous challenges that emerge during the *PID/PA* stage. Consultants must clarify high-inference consultee language, including guiding the problem-solving beyond surface-level problem descriptors, and avoid the temptation to prematurely intervene or prescribe solutions. By working through the numerous activities provided in this chapter, and bearing in mind the chapter's six Big Ideas, we hope you will feel more prepared to accurately identify and understand problems in collaboration with your consultee, thus boosting your chances for subsequent intervention success.

8

DESIGNING AND IMPLEMENTING INTERVENTIONS

It's Not Magic—It's Planning, Monitoring, and Performance Feedback

Those who plan do better than those who do not plan, even should they rarely stick to their plan.

However beautiful the strategy, you should occasionally look at the results.

(Winston Churchill)

In this chapter, we overview two stages of problem-solving related to interventions: (1) *Intervention Planning*, and (2) *Intervention Implementation, Monitoring, and Performance Feedback*. Before moving too far along, consider your own prior experiences with interventions in schools.

ACTIVITY 8.1 (INDIVIDUAL)

Warm-Up Questions: Intervention Stages

Think about an intervention that you have designed and implemented or observed during any school-based experience you have had thus far in your professional training or in practice. Write down reflections on your prior experiences with interventions in schools. You can write down sentences or just key words.

1. Was the intervention successful? Why or why not?
2. What did you learn about designing, implementing, and evaluating interventions?

One lesson we have learned over our combined years of consulting and supervising consultation is that *interventions are not magic, and consultants are not magicians.* Careful planning is necessary for implementation to occur with fidelity. It is essential for the consultant and consultee to continue to work together during this stage (Noell, Volz, Henderson, & Williams, 2017). First of all, as stated in Big Idea #1 in Chapter 7, complex problems such as those that arise in schools rarely have simple solutions. Even interventions that boast an excellent evidence base will not work for every child in every context and may not work instantly or may lose their effects over time. Secondly, interventions are not implemented with the flick of a magic wand. It takes effort, time, flexibility, and collaboration to put an intervention into place, to keep it working successfully, and to achieve behavior maintenance and generalization. This is even truer when the intervention is designed to impact more than one student, a group, or a school. Even in baseball, according to the New York Mets' general manager, "What differentiates teams now is not the ability to comprehend new ideas, … but the ability to implement those new ideas throughout an organization." Whether in schools or in baseball, effective implementation is the holy grail of consultation.

During the *Intervention Planning* stage of problem-solving, the consultation dyad establishes an appropriate intervention, one based on the identified problem from the *Problem Identification and Problem Analysis (PID/PA)* stage, to implement, and determines who will implement the intervention as well as when, where, and how often it will be implemented. Subsequently, through ongoing data review and discussion during the *Intervention Implementation, Monitoring, and Performance Feedback* stage of problem-solving, the consultant and consultee consider what is working and what is not working with the intervention and what steps to take next. This chapter overviews more specifically what is to be accomplished during each of these two problem-solving stages. Consultation processes that facilitate successful stage navigation are also highlighted. Several real examples and activities are integrated throughout the chapter to enhance your knowledge and skills during these two stages.

The Nuts and Bolts of Intervention Design

In the *Intervention Design* stage of problem-solving, the consultant and consultee select an intervention that matches with the baseline problem established during *PID/PA*. An overview of the "business" of intervention design is provided in Table 8.1.

In Video 8.1, Dr. Elise Pas discusses the implementation process and its intersection with the problem-solving skills we have been presenting.

TABLE 8.1 An Overview of the Intervention Design Stage of Problem-Solving

Stage	Purpose	Business to Be Accomplished
Intervention Design	Collaboratively develop instructional and/or behavioral management strategies targeting goals	Elicit consultee's ideas/strategies Discuss: *What* classroom-based strategy will meet goals? *Where* will strategy be implemented? *When* can strategy be implemented? *How often* will strategy be implemented? *Who* will be responsible? Consider conditions to create/maintain instructional match Consider if multiple students can benefit from the intervention Document specifics of what, when, how often, and who

EBIs and ebis

Interventions may be selected from a number of pre-existing academic, behavioral, or social-emotional programs with manualized curricula and strong foundations of evidence. We term them here Evidence-Based Interventions (uppercase EBI). Alternatively, the consultant and consultee may collaboratively design an intervention based on strong evidence-based principles underlying effective prevention or treatment, that is *kernels*, of behavior (e.g., Embry & Biglan, 2008) or instruction (e.g., Ysseldyke & Christenson, 2002) targeted to match student needs and the consultee's instructional context. We term these interventions evidence-based interventions (lowercase ebi). Both EBIs and ebis are informed by empirical data, making them research-based interventions that can be appropriate to incorporate in consultative problem-solving. Some examples of consultation interventions implemented by consultants-in-training (CITs) and teacher consultees during a recent semester of consultation training are provided in Table 8.2.

Intervention Flexibility

Table 8.2 contains both EBIs and ebis, and references modifications made to interventions when they were implemented. When interventions are adapted to fit the individualized context of implementation, they achieve "*flexibility within fidelity*" (Kendall & Beidas, 2007), thereby enhancing the likelihood of intervention acceptability, adherence, and success. Flexibility within fidelity also can increase cultural responsiveness within school consultation problem-solving (Sander, Hernandez Finch, & Newell, 2016). We acknowledge that it is tricky to balance between being flexible and staying true to an EBI protocol (Simon, 2016). However, the intervention stages of problem-solving require school consultants to be critical

TABLE 8.2 Examples of Interventions in Consultation Cases during a Recently Instructed School Consultation Course

---

Pre-teaching and reviewing vocabulary from Story Town curriculum

"Drill sandwich" to teach sight words

"Drill sandwich" for letter sounds and sound blends; adapted to include "speed naming" for known sounds, teacher-made stories, and more direct instruction

Planned Discussion with student regarding disruptive behavior, combined with verbal praise from teacher, self-monitoring, and reward motivator

Supporting teacher to implement the CHAMPs Program

Coordinating carpet space for a "bigger" kindergarten student so he wouldn't bother peers, discussion with student about boundaries, teaching behavior through examples/non-examples

Classroom setup rearrangement (e.g., no kids in back of teacher)

Sticker reward, with immediacy and frequent review, to combat refusal behavior/reward compliance

Point system with rewards

Stickers to promote on-task behavior

Xtra Math online math intervention

Behavior Intervention Plan with "mini-interventions" at Antecedents, Behavior (e.g., Instructional strategies), and Consequence stages

Clarifying step-by-step oral directions (original problem was "too many redirections") by providing written list on whiteboard at the student's desk

Visual checklist as a reminder of things to take home from school/bring to school

Previewing vocabulary with individual student, and as intervention progressed, whole class

---

thinkers during intervention design and implementation rather than overly rigid, robotic, or prescriptive, keeping in mind the critical design element(s) when adapting an intervention to the context in which implementation will occur. In one vocabulary intervention adopted by a school, teachers had students keep a word box on their desk for new words but did not implement correctly the recommended number of new words per week that students were required to learn, leading to a lack of progress for many of them (Rosenfield & Rubinson, 1985).

Social Validity

In addition to being flexible, interventions should be socially valid. Social validity refers to the social significance of the intervention goals and outcomes as well as the acceptability and feasibility of implementation (Bailey & Burch, 2017; Wolf, 1978). Questions for consideration regarding social validity include:

How valuable is this intervention to stakeholders (e.g., teachers, parents, students)?

Are the target variables important to stakeholders?

Are the target variables meaningful?

Is the intervention acceptable to the consultee?

Social validity may be assessed via consumer ratings (e.g., interviewing or surveying consultees) and also by comparing student performance to peer norms (e.g., is the intervention helping the student perform more like typically performing peers?).

Collaborative Design

The process of selecting or designing an intervention should be collaborative. The notion of collaborative intervention design is actually introduced in consultation during *Contracting* (see Chapter 6) and is further catalyzed through the establishment of a shared problem definition during *PID/PA*. It is appropriate for you to bring to an *Intervention Planning* consultation session some ideas for potential interventions, and you likely will have ideas given your specialized knowledge base as a school consultant. However, providing a list of interventions and saying "choose one" is not the best approach to intervention design. Nor is prescribing an intervention without eliciting sufficient consultee input. The intervention you think is best may not be feasible within the classroom context; it may be too time- or other resource-consuming; or the teacher may have attempted the intervention previously and found it to be ineffective.

Teacher input into intervention selection increases the likelihood of intervention adherence, meaning the plan is more likely to be implemented as designed. For example, Dart, Cook, Collins, Gresham, and Chenier (2012) investigated outcomes when teachers "test drove" interventions, that is, tried them out for a brief duration during behavioral consultation. The researchers found that intervention plan adherence increased when preferred interventions were selected, as did student academic engaged time. An excerpt from an actual *Intervention Planning* dialogue is provided in Activity 8.2, along with some questions for consideration to help you reflect on the role of collaboration during this stage of problem-solving.

ACTIVITY 8.2 (INDIVIDUAL, GROUP)

Intervention Acceptability

The following is an actual excerpt from an Intervention Planning session in which a consultant and consultee discussed a second grader's lack of instructional match in math assignments, which also seemed to be problematic for several other students. Review the transcript and answer the subsequent questions individually and, if possible, compare responses with a partner or in a small group.

> **Teacher Consultee (TC):** She is in here for afternoon math. It's hard to give her any individual attention. We do as much as we can.

> **Consultant (C):** Yeah, during their math worksheets, you are typically walking around a little bit, right?

TC: Right, right.

C: And you discuss if the students have any questions and things like that.

TC: Right.

C: And I know that when you are assigning the work to the students, you ask them to take out their notebooks and rip out a page. Is that right?

TC: Yeah.

C: So how do you think we can make [packets aligned with their instructional level in math] something that we can make simple enough to do in the classroom and on a daily basis?

TC: It's so hard... And maybe [the students] get 30 seconds of me saying, "go back and correct this problem or that." Then they go back to their seat and copy off someone else's paper, then bring it back up, and oh, okay, now it's right.

C: I'm hearing what you're saying because you're saying that you don't have a lot of time.

TC: Yeah, and I know it's my job...

C: Yes, that that's why we are sitting here and trying to brainstorm what we can do here in the classroom for these students. I'm just wondering how much time it would save if you were able to pull them aside for a couple of minutes and just give them a quick run-down of what they as a small group would be going over. Versus them each coming up individually and you giving them each individual feedback ... and it is sporadic and disjointed, and then they don't even do the work as you described. Does that make sense?

TC: Yeah.

C: Is that something you'd be willing to try?

TC: Who's going to put the packet together? Me?

C: Well, that's something that we can do together and obviously with the special education teacher.

TC: And when? Everyday? What time?

C: I understand you feel you don't have a lot of time.

TC: It just becomes hard to be consistent...

C: So here's the thing with the packets: I would be willing to work with the special education teacher to put these together if you would be willing to discuss it with them for a couple of minutes after you give the whole group math lesson.

TC: Sure, yeah.

Questions for Reflection:

1. Given this brief excerpt, how acceptable do you think this intervention idea is to the teacher? How do you know?

2. How would you guess intervention acceptability demonstrated through this excerpt relates to the *PID/PA* process the dyad had previously engaged in?

3. What consultant and consultee actions might be useful to increase intervention acceptability?

Detailing and Documenting the Intervention

Interventions consist of:

- a *what* (i.e., a strategy to meet goals),
- a *where* (i.e., intervention setting),
- a *when* (i.e., time of day for implementation),
- a *how often* (i.e., frequency of implementation), and
- a *who* (i.e., person or persons responsible for implementation).

Each of these aspects of the intervention can be documented on a tool such as the Student Documentation Form (SDF) referenced in Chapter 7.

However, in practice, we have found discussions of interventions are often vague, relying on one or a few of these details without the others, or not fully specifying a protocol for implementation. Plans such as, "She can go with Carole [the reading specialist] during that time," or, "he gets reading help during homeroom—that should be sufficient," are unclear intervention plans. Describing the intervention in detail allows the consultant and consultee to work out logistical kinks, thereby enhancing the likelihood of treatment adherence and intervention effectiveness. Further, students who are discussed in consultations often have other interventions in place to support them, and communication with other resource providers about intervention details, including schedules, can help streamline intervention strategies. A real example of a poorly defined intervention plan is provided in Activity 8.3, with a chance for you to reflect on consequences of this plan.

ACTIVITY 8.3 (INDIVIDUAL, GROUP)

The Homework Club

Read the following case example. Answer the subsequent questions individually and, if possible, compare responses with a partner or in a small group.

Sophia is a school psychologist intern participating on a middle school problem-solving team. Many of the students that are discussed by the team are assigned to an after-school homework club in lieu of other interventions. Although it is primarily geared towards students struggling academically (in any subject), the team sometimes prescribes the homework club for students with non-academic issues. Although it is clear the group meets at 4:00 PM after school, other details, such as what instructional support strategies are applied, which personnel support which students, and other logistics, are unclear. Additionally, the homework tutors rely on students to indicate which assignments/academic areas they need support with even though many of these students are struggling with problems such as poor organization and not logging assignments in their homework agenda books. When Sophia asked some teachers "off the record" about their perceptions of the homework club, all reported the group wasn't effective in increasing students' academic skills.

Questions for Reflection:

1. What are some of the problems with the homework club intervention?
2. How might this intervention be redesigned to be more effective?

Who Will Implement the Intervention?

Detailing who will implement the intervention is particularly important. Traditional descriptions of consultation put the consultee in the roles of plan designer and executor (e.g., Kratochwill & Bergan, 1990), roles consistent with the indirect nature of consultative service delivery. However, consultees may enter the consultation relationship with a mistaken assumption that the consultant will shoulder the responsibility for direct services, such as assessing the student for special education eligibility evaluation or providing a pullout intervention for the student without the consultee's involvement. Sometimes consultants inadvertently reinforce this perception through frequent usage of "I" language (e.g., I will assess, I will observe, I will determine, I will provide), or through actions such as being prescriptive regarding intervention design or taking full ownership of intervention implementation. Activity 8.4 provides an example of an implicit struggle over intervention ownership between a CIT and a consultee about a seventh-grade student.

ACTIVITY 8.4 (INDIVIDUAL, GROUP)

Who Owns the Intervention?

The following is an excerpt from an actual consultation session focused on intervention design between a consultant and consultee about a seventh-grade student named Luis. Read this interchange and answer the subsequent questions individually and, if possible, compare responses with a partner or in a small group

> **CIT:** Okay, so one of the things I was thinking might work for Luis, and this again, I want to keep this as collaborative as possible, is having

some sort of self-monitoring tool for him, so you know we can have the definition of what it means to follow teacher directions, classroom directions, what it means to follow through with directions and also have some sort of rewards, structured reward plan, as well as consequences that are embedded in the plan. And when I say consequences, I mean things that you can easily implement within the classroom that wouldn't take time, and it wouldn't be distracting and something that you know, we can even start off with it being during his 20-minute warm-up you know for a week and leave it at that. And if he's self-monitoring, we can set a criterion for how many points he would have to earn either that week or that day in order to get some sort of reward. And if he was not doing it, what kind of consequence would be part of that, and you know, you can agree, disagree, you know if you have any thoughts on how that might work.

Teacher Consultee (TC): Um, I'm just not good with um papers and contracts, I'm really not good—and I'm open for anything, but I…

CIT: Okay, well this is kind of what I was thinking about, okay? And I can talk to him, pull him or teach him, but if it was something along the lines of this [I'm showing her a self-monitoring graph example], you know that he can have, if they were half sheets of paper he can have in his room or on his desk, we can laminate it, Velcro it, you know have it be dry erase; it doesn't matter—something that he can easily keep track of it himself and be able to see, so it's not necessarily you watching him, it's him watching him.

Questions for Reflection

1. How did the consultant attempt to be collaborative in this brief interchange? Was it successful? Why or why not?
2. In what ways might the consultant have approached this conversation differently?
3. If the consultee agreed to a version of this intervention, what would you predict about the eventual implementation process?

In contemporary school settings it is indeed likely that the consultant has some sort of direct contact with the student (Gutkin & Curtis, 2009). However, it is essential to remember that consultation is provided with the intention of *giving psychology away* (Miller, 1969) to the consultee, teaching him or her how to fish rather than supplying the fish. Therefore, the consultant must strike a balance between providing support to solve the problem and taking full ownership of the problem. The consultant's involvement in intervention implementation should be designed with adult learning principles (Joyce & Showers, 2002) and professional development frameworks (Desimone & Garet, 2015) in mind (see Chapter 1, Figure 1.1), thereby positioning consultation as a form of embedded professional development for consultees.

For example, in Ingham Intermediate School District in Michigan, consultation support is provided for teachers regarding the research-based instructional strategies of increasing opportunities for student responding; formative assessment; effective feedback for students; and systematic problem-solving (Barrett, Newman, & Hazel, 2018). Not only do school consultants discuss the research base of these strategies and an implementation plan with teachers, they also gather baseline data regarding instructional practices, model the new practices, and scaffold the teacher's as they integrate them into their instruction. Given the collaborative relationship between consultants and teachers, the processes have been viewed by the teachers in the district as supportive and helpful, and the data demonstrate increased implementation of research-based instruction. The implementation of Instructional Consultation Teams provides another example of the relationship of consultation and adult learning principles; see Rosenfield and Gravois (1996).

Intervening With More Than One Student

Interventions are often implemented within the context of multi-tiered systems of support (MTSS) in schools (Walker & Shinn, 2010). As discussed elsewhere in this text, although sometimes an individual student surfaces as the focus of consultation, multiple students can often benefit from the support provided by the teacher. In other words, many Tier 3 concerns can actually better be framed as Tier 2 or Tier 1 concerns relevant to a classroom, grade level, or even school building. Such reframes often allow you and the consultee to move from a focus on an individual student's pathology towards an ecologically-framed problem situated in school. For example, you might think aloud with the consultee: "I am wondering if some of the other students in Noah's reading group would also benefit from previewing the vocabulary. What do you think?" Asking the consultee directly about broader intervention applicability would also be appropriate, for example: "Are there other students who might benefit from re-teaching the expectations of morning meeting?"

The Nuts and Bolts of Intervention

Implementation, Monitoring, and Performance Feedback

Following *Intervention Planning*, it is time to put the plan into action during the *Intervention Implementation, Monitoring, and Performance Feedback* stage. An overview

TABLE 8.3 An Overview of the Intervention Implementation, Monitoring, and Performance Feedback Stage of Problem-Solving

Stage	Purpose	Business to be Accomplished
Intervention Implementation, Monitoring, and Performance Feedback	Ensure intervention adherence/ accurate implementation of intervention	Continue meeting while intervention is being implemented Clarify what's working and what needs refining Elicit consultee's perception of progress Provide performance feedback regarding level of adherence to intervention, with consideration given to implementation changes as needed Collaboratively review and discuss data Compare progress with goals

of the "business" of this stage is provided in Table 8.3. Several steps can be taken to ensure that the plan is delivered completely and appropriately.

Ongoing Meetings

The consultation dyad should continue to meet during this stage of problem-solving (Noell et al., 2017; Rosenfield, 2014). Although this might seem like an obvious point, we have observed time and again consultants or problem-solving teams prescribing interventions for teachers to implement and then leaving the teachers for multiple weeks to do so without providing further support. When the intervention is not implemented as intended, the consultee may be unfairly labeled as "resistant" or "disinterested" when "unsupported" would be a more appropriate descriptor. Research has confirmed that "in the absence of effective programming to support implementation, implementation is often poor and deteriorates over time (Noell et al., 2017, p. 525). There is also evidence that quality implementation, as one would suspect, is related to positive outcomes for students (Noell et al., 2017).

But what happens during the meetings is the critical factor. Continuous contact between the consultant and consultee allows for reviewing data (i.e., progress monitoring), assessing what is and is not working for the consultee and student via collaborative data review, and discussing any necessary tweaks to the intervention or implementation plan (i.e., performance feedback). These features of the meetings are essential to implementation quality.

Meetings during this stage may occur less frequently than in earlier stages of problem-solving and also tend to be briefer in nature, as they focus on "fine tuning" the intervention as needed. We recommend beginning this stage of problem-solving by meeting with your usual frequency (e.g., weekly or more frequently) and thinning the meeting schedule (biweekly, and then monthly) consistent with data indicating the intervention's continued success *and* the consultee's comfort with receiving reduced support.

Progress Monitoring

Two types of monitoring occur while the intervention is being implemented: Monitoring the student's progress and monitoring the plan's implementation (Kratochwill & Bergan, 1990). With respect to monitoring student progress, intervention outcome data can be compared to baseline data and goals established during *PID/PA*. Consistent with descriptions of goal setting in Chapter 7, consultation interventions will ideally result in both student growth and a reduction in the performance gap between the student or students and typically performing peers. Although beyond the scope of this chapter, single case design methods are quite applicable to monitoring consultation outcomes given the focus on individual or small groups of students; interested readers are referred to Kazdin (2011) for more information on single case designs.

With respect to monitoring the intervention plan, gathering data on treatment adherence is essential, because if a plan is not implemented as intended, it is a non-event, and it is impossible to conclude whether a student is responsive to the intervention. A checklist of intervention steps may be helpful to measure adherence and also as a reference tool to support implementation (e.g., see Schussler, 2012; also, an example of an intervention script and adherence checklists can be found in Appendix E). Direct observation, permanent products, and self-report provide useful approaches to gather data regarding treatment adherence.

Performance Feedback

A robust research base focused on performance feedback in consultation indicates that ongoing meetings between the consultant and consultee serve to enhance intervention adherence (Fallon, Collier-Meek, Maggin, Sanetti, & Johnson, 2015). Performance feedback is more easily delivered within the context of a collaborative relationship developed during earlier stages of problem-solving. Also, Noell et al. (2017) found it was effective to integrate a commitment emphasis with performance feedback, including the following prior to implementation:

> The consultant described how it is common for us to plan to change our behavior, but fail to follow through due to competing demands and ingrained habits … the teacher and consultant discussed proactive steps the teacher could choose to take to support implementation …. Teachers were free to devise any strategy they thought would be helpful or no strategy at all.
>
> *(p. 532)*

Performance feedback meetings include a discussion of what is going well and what is not going well with the intervention, with reference to treatment adherence and student outcome data (Sanetti, Fallon, & Collier-Meek, 2013).

CITs are sometimes concerned about providing performance feedback, as doing so may seem critical of the consultee if the intervention is not working. However, in such instances, performance feedback can be viewed as an opportunity for perspective taking: discussing with the consultee what is not working, why, and what can be done to improve implementation. Of course, such a conversation is more easily done within a functioning collaborative relationship, as mentioned above. In Activity 8.5, an excerpt from a CIT's supervision process log is provided for your consideration of challenges in providing performance feedback to consultees.

ACTIVITY 8.5 (INDIVIDUAL, GROUP)

Performance Feedback

The following is a part of a reflection from a consultant-in-training (CIT) who was consulting with a kindergarten teacher, Ms. Young, to support a student named Sal. She is describing challenges faced during progress monitoring and performance feedback and requesting supervision advice. Read the reflection and answer the subsequent questions individually. If possible, compare responses with a partner or in a small group.

CIT Reflection:

We are progress monitoring and still meeting weekly to see how the intervention is going. I have gone into the classroom many times and have noticed that the interventions are not going exactly how I wish they would. The timer that we were setting for Sal was not working properly, and Ms. Young [the consultee] seemed a little confused about reinforcing Sal. These issues were what we talked about in our meeting ... It seems as though the intervention addressing latency (getting Sal to start working right away) is not working according to Ms. Young's data. I think Ms. Young is not implementing the timer intervention exactly how we talked about, because the timer is not working correctly, and our data are inconsistent from each other. I also feel as though she is worried about collecting data on Sal that shows that interventions are not working.

She has a team meeting to address Sal's needs next week, and I feel as though she wants to collect as much data about Sal's difficulties and not focus on the intervention. In the consultation session, Ms. Young showed me the idea she had to change one of the interventions. Every 2 minutes the timer goes off, if Sal was working then he gets a sticker. There are four stickers, and then Sal gets to go to the treasure chest.

I thought this was a great idea! She explained that Sal has only gotten one sticker, and it is really hard for him to stay on task for 2 minutes and get a sticker. We talked about how the timer is not working properly, and that may be why it seems the intervention is not working. I explained the importance of making sure Sal is successful and making sure he gets a sticker every 2 minutes. We decided to try the intervention again. We are going to continue with interventions and see how they go. I plan to go in two days per week to work individually with Sal. If these interventions don't work, I will feel very frustrated and disheartened. I think Ms. Young believes that Sal needs an aide with him at all times to be successful in school and that our efforts are not enough. I definitely feel like a behavior plan would benefit Sal, and I hope to see him stay in the classroom.

We will continue to use our interventions, hoping that the timer will work and that Ms. Young now knows when and how to reinforce Sal's good behaviors. Maybe I can show her how to use the chart correctly with a timer that works. What are your suggestions for how to use communication skills better when Ms. Young says things like, "He laid on the floor for 45 minutes today," or, "He can't even work for two minutes, and I can't keep monitoring him because I have a whole class!"? This is a tough first case!

Questions for Reflection:

1. Summarize the concerns that the consultant has regarding intervention implementation.
2. Given those concerns, how might she provide performance feedback to the consultee?
3. What thoughts would you have as the consultant's supervisor or as a peer support? What additional information might help you provide feedback to support this consultant?

Summary

Intervening with teachers on behalf of students is a critical component of the School Consultation process. In this chapter, we have reviewed two stages: *Intervention Planning*, and *Intervention Implementation, Monitoring, and Performance Feedback*. The stages are collaborative and systematic. Consultants and consultees work together to: select a socially valid intervention matched to the problem(s) defined during *PID/PA*; clarify all details of an implementation plan, including what, where, when, how often, and who; and attend to intervention integrity or adherence, including the potential need for flexibility within fidelity.

As posited earlier, *interventions are not magic* (even EBIs!), *and consultants are not magicians*. Therefore, despite the natural tendency consultants might have to provide immediate help, and the reinforcement consultants might receive from consultees to provide a quick fix, doing so might actually derail the consultation process. After reading the chapter and completing the activities embedded within, we hope you feel more prepared to navigate the numerous challenges that emerge during these problem-solving stages.

9
POST-INTERVENTION PLANNING AND CLOSURE

Every new beginning comes from some other beginning's end.

(*Seneca*)

In this chapter we explore the *Post-Intervention Planning and Closure (PIPC)* stage of problem-solving in school consultation. We highlight strategies to facilitate successful case closure, including consideration given to consultation goals both for clients (i.e., students) and consultees. Before we begin, take a moment to consider these questions:

ACTIVITY 9.1 (INDIVIDUAL)

Warm-Up Questions: Post-Intervention Planning and Closure

Write down your assumptions about closing out a consultation case. You can write down sentences or just key words.

1. When is a consultation complete? How do you know?
2. Which variables are important to consider when closing out a consultation?

These questions are trickier to answer than they might first appear. First of all, even if a problem is technically solved according to the data (i.e., long-term goals are met and gaps between students and typical peers are closed), the consultant and consultee need to determine which aspects of the intervention will remain in place, which will be eliminated or faded as the consultation comes to a close, and how behavioral generalization and maintenance will be achieved. Second, consultees may also have an additional problem they wish to work on with the consultant that has not been directly addressed through this initial consultation. Third, a consultation may come to an abrupt end even if the problem is not solved. For example, the school year may have ended; a student may have moved; the teacher may be taking a maternity leave; a teacher may have lost interest in the consultation, or not have further time to devote to it; or the student has not made academic or behavioral progress despite ongoing consultation efforts. Finally, school consultation is also more than a series of problem-solving steps. It is a complex process with embedded interpersonal interactions at its heart. Therefore, closing out a consultation requires attention to the consultation relationship.

The Nuts and Bolts of Post-Intervention Planning and Closure

Scant conceptual literature or empirical research has focused on the final stage of consultation (Dougherty, Tack, Fullam, & Hammer, 1996). When it is referenced, the formal conclusion of consultation has been called closure (Rosenfield, 2014); disengagement (including four phases: evaluating, post-consultation planning, reducing involvement and following up, and terminating; Dougherty, 2013); post-intervention planning (Kratochwill et al., 2014); and termination (Gallesich, 1982). We term the stage as *PIPC*, a title that indicates consultation (a) does not end with intervention selection, implementation, or evaluation; (b) needs to be systematically rather than haphazardly resolved or left hanging; and (c) has, at its core, a formal relationship that needs to be concluded. An overview of the "business" of the *PIPC* stage is provided in Table 9.1.

A first consideration regarding closing out the consultation is whether or not consultation goals are met. Progress monitoring during the previous problem-solving stage served the purpose of formative assessment. In *PIPC*, the consultant and consultee engage in summative assessment by measuring present levels of performance on target variables compared to long-term goals. Graphic representations of the data are helpful in analyzing progress and making decisions regarding goal achievement.

In addition to student goals, you and the consultee may have goals for the consultee regarding intervention ownership and knowledge and skill development; this is a second consideration in closing out a consultation. As articulated elsewhere in this text, consultee professional learning is part of the purpose of School Consultation (SC). Consultees can gain new knowledge, skills, confidence, and objectivity to support their future work (Kaiser, Rosenfield, & Gravois, 2009). Therefore, assessing the consultee's professional learning as well as efficacy in implementing the intervention now and in the future are part of the *PIPC* stage. This can take the form of verbal report during a consultation interview or ratings

TABLE 9.1 An Overview of the *Post-Intervention Planning and Closure* Stage of Problem-Solving

Stage	Purpose	Business to Be Accomplished
Post-Intervention Planning and Closure	Formally conclude the consultation relationship regarding the targeted concern	Close if (a) goals are met; (b) consultee can implement independently if needed; (c) strategies are fading/faded
		Elicit consultee's plans to maintain student progress
		Determine documentation of efforts
		Consider addressing other priority areas not yet addressed (and return to *PID/PA* for new priority concern)
		If case is explicitly closed, let consultee know how support can be accessed in the future
		Communicate with parents, colleagues, teams as needed

of social validity. Open-ended questions can help stimulate discussion regarding the consultee's professional learning and overall experience in consultation. Examples of such open-ended reflection questions are provided in Table 9.2. The consultee's willingness to reflect on the consultation process may be facilitated by your own willingness to share your experiences as the consultant. You should genuinely reflect on any challenges faced but also emphasize positives such as student progress made as a result of the consultation and things you learned from working with the consultee.

A third consideration in closing out the consultation is if, when, and how to fade intervention strategies that are currently in place. For example, a school psychologist consultant worked with several eighth-grade teachers to more frequently acknowledge positive peer-to-peer interactions in the classroom. The consultant and consultees planned how to thin out the reinforcement schedule over time yet continue to acknowledge student behaviors in the future. Some interventions may remain fully intact after the consultation ends, such as added instructional techniques supporting multiple students in a third-grade classroom (e.g., previewing unfamiliar vocabulary before reading a new story). Others may

TABLE 9.2 Examples of Open-Ended Reflection Questions a Consultant May Ask During PIPC

- What are your thoughts on this consulting experience?
- What changes, if any, have you noticed with the student since we started working together?
- Have we accomplished what we set out to do?
- What, if anything, have you learned from working together?
- What will happen after our consultation ends?

be fully removed after goals have been accomplished, such as a planned discussion with a student about homework completion that immediately solved the problem. Regardless of whether interventions strategies remain as they are, are altered, or are eliminated, a discussion of how student progress will be maintained should occur.

Since consultation encompasses a data-based problem-solving process, the consultation efforts and their results should be documented. Visual representations of baseline data, goal-setting, progress monitoring, and summative results provide strong evidence of the process. It may also be helpful for you to create a format for documenting your collaborative efforts or to write an email or letter to the consultee containing the details of the intervention and highlighting the progress made by the student(s) (see Figure 9.1 for an example of a letter). Such a written document can be particularly useful before a disruption in the school calendar, such as prior to winter or summer break. The Student Documentation Form (SDF), found in Appendix D and described earlier in this text, provides another example that documents most of the aspects of the problem-solving process described here. The school in which you are consulting might have its own system to document consultative problem-solving efforts. If so, you might consider whether that procedure documents all components of the process.

Sometimes intervention efforts that were successful with a student during one school year are not implemented at the beginning of the next school year, or efforts that were unsuccessful are futilely repeated the following year. Providing information about the intervention to parents, next year's teachers, colleagues who will work with that student, and/or school problem-solving teams can increase the likelihood that support for the student will be jumpstarted in the future. Documenting successes and sharing that information with key stakeholders can also act to increase support for future consultative service delivery in the school.

In the *Problem Identification and Problem Analysis (PID/PA)* stage of problem-solving, you and the consultee may have prioritized one problem, putting other issues to the side. During *PIPC* you can revisit the previously defined problems to see if any are still in need of attention or if any new issues have arisen. Often the focus on a pivotal issue during the consultation eliminates the other problems that the teacher initially experienced, such as when gaining academic skills increases academic engagement, work completion, and mitigates problem behavior. Sometimes additional problems remain to be addressed. In such instances, revisiting the *PID/PA* stage of problem-solving will be necessary, cycling back through the full problem-solving process for the concern to be addressed.

Just as entry and *Contracting* sets the stage for how consultation will ensue, *PIPC* determines how it will conclude *and* how it will be accessed in the future. Therefore, a final key component of the *PIPC* stage is making sure consultees know the door is open for future consultations and are aware of how to access future support (Dougherty et al., 1996; Rosenfield, 2014). This is particularly important for internal school consultants given that relationships with

Example of a Transition Letter

Dear Ms. Smith,

As I prepare to complete my practicum experience at Flintstone Elementary, I wanted to take an opportunity to summarize our consultation case, thus far. We have been working to develop the sight word vocabulary of a student in your class so that he will meet the district-wide, grade level goal for the number of known sight words by the end of this school year. Based on initial information that we collected about Angelo's reading skills, we determined that he had mastered the first 25 words on the sight word list. Therefore, we decided to focus our efforts on assisting Angelo in mastering the next 50 words on the list. Baseline data revealed that Angelo could read between 70% and 85% of the 50 identified words. You felt that Angelo could learn all of the words by the end of the school year, so we set the goal at 100% mastery.

We decided to use an "incremental rehearsal" technique to assist Angelo in learning the words that he did not know. This intervention lowers frustration because both known and unknown words are included. You also came up with the great idea of incorporating some of the unknown words into Angelo's spelling list each week. Since these interventions have been implemented, we have seen a steady and consistent improvement in the percentage of words that Angelo can read automatically. Angelo has increased his percentage of known words from 70% to 94%. He is very close to his goal of 100%!

As we agreed during our last meeting, you will continue to use the interventions with Angelo until he meets his goal. Clyde, the school psychologist, will meet with you for the remainder of this year about your work with Angelo. Clyde is also aware of the possibility of implementing a behavioral intervention with Angelo, and that there are other students in your class that may also benefit from academic or behavioral interventions.

I really enjoyed working with you this year and am confident that we have made a positive impact on Angelo's reading skills. Thank you for all of your effort and assistance throughout the consultation process. I hope that you found the experience beneficial and rewarding, and that you will continue to seek out consultation as necessary. Good luck with the rest of the school year and in the future.

Thank You,

Rose Johnson,
School Psychology Intern

FIGURE 9.1   Example of a transition letter.

consultees such as teachers are ongoing. Therefore, although the *consultation case* may be closed, the *consultation relationship* remains open for future collaborative problem-solving.

In Video 9.1, Dr. Arlene Silva summarizes the issues around this stage.

Closing Words on Closure: Leaving an Open Door

To end this chapter, we offer some final thoughts on the importance of this under-studied and under-emphasized consultation stage. You may be thinking that engaging in closure could be awkward. However, just as in romantic relationships, closure in consultation may be considered a form of respect. Leaving a consultation hanging without a formal conclusion is disrespectful to the consultee and may deter the consultee's future willingness to access consultation supports (Dougherty et al., 1996). Instead, explicit closure acknowledges your joint work and sets the stage for future consultations with this consultee as well as with other consultees in the system. In other words, closing the door on one consultation opens the doors to others.

10

LEARNING TO CONSULT

The Roles of Assessment, Feedback, and Deliberate Practice

Becoming is better than being.

(Carol Dweck)

It is not enough to simply engage in consultation experiences as a novice to become competent in the domain. The literature on developing expertise (e.g., Ericsson, 2009; Ericsson & Pool, 2016) helps us to understand why. As has been detailed for psychotherapist supervision, training, and professional development (Rousmaniere, Goodyear, Miller, & Wampold, 2017), we propose that the development of consultation competency and expertise requires a cyclic process of:

- Assessing a baseline of knowledge and skills, including strengths and skills in need of improvement;
- Obtaining systematic, ongoing, and formal feedback from a knowledgeable other (e.g., a supervisor or mentor); and
- Engaging in the deliberate practice of consultation.

These components can be thought of as a three-legged stool, each leg essential and reliant on the others to support the development of consultation competency. But it is important to acknowledge that no matter how many hours you work at developing your consultation skills, without supervision feedback linked to direct observations/assessments of performance, you are not likely to hone your skills for effective and efficient practice in the complex context of the schools.

Earlier in Chapter 7, we presented Caplan's (1970) four types of consultee problems: lack of knowledge, lack of skill, lack of objectivity, and lack of self-confidence. These are also problem areas for the consultant-in-training (CIT). While we have focused on the first two, knowledge and skill, it is important also to remember that CITs can also experience a lack of self-confidence or a lack of objectivity.

In Chapter 6, we alluded to the lack of self-confidence that a CIT might feel when contracting to consult with more experienced staff members in a school and the strategy of "acting as if" one were competent. But this lack of self-confidence can also emerge at later points in the process. Here, supervision can be helpful in providing support (see Vaganek, 2012, for an example of lack of self-confidence and the support of supervision around this issue). Similarly, CITs can experience a lack of objectivity in working on a consultation process, and supervision and feedback are necessary to help the CIT recognize when that is occurring. For example, Pickering (2012), through supervision, came to recognize his loss of objectivity in his work with the teacher. It is critical to remember that along with lack of knowledge and skill, lack of objectivity and self-confidence are also barriers to competent performance as a consultant.

Assessing Consultation Knowledge and Skills

The first leg in the stool of consultation competency development is the assessment of your knowledge and skills, including strengths and weaknesses. Consultation is a complex domain to evaluate. Three interrelated areas may be the focus of evaluation: (1) consultation content knowledge, (2) consultation process skills, and (3) consultation outcomes (i.e., what impact you have on the consultees and clients you are serving).

Evaluating Consultation Content Knowledge

There is some agreement as to what the body of school consultation content knowledge consists of, much of which is embodied in this text. The National Association of School Psychologists (2010b) specifies Consultation and Collaboration as a key competency domain and provides examples of professional practices (see Chapter 1, Table 1.3); Division 13 of the APA (2017) has published consultation competency guidelines that are relevant to school consultation competency development and could inform evaluation. Burkhouse (2012) provided a specific example of an evaluation tool that measures both content knowledge and process skills specifically for Instructional Consultation (IC; see Appendix F). In addition, this scale is aligned with the developmental model of training described elsewhere in this text, since it includes levels of skill acquisition. Another tool, developed and psychometrically validated by Guiney, Harris, Zusho, and Cancelli (2014; see Appendix G), can be used to measure self-efficacy for consultation. Consultation content knowledge emerges within a graduate classroom setting, largely focused on awareness or conceptual understanding. To move beyond conceptual understanding towards application of skills in action requires sufficient exposure to content combined with opportunities for simulated practice, application in real school contexts, and supervision.

Evaluating Consultation Process Skills

Process skills such as strategic communication and relationship building are trickier to evaluate than content knowledge. There are particular supervision strategies that are most helpful to objectively assess such processes. First, live observations or audio- or video-recordings of consultations provide direct information about the application of skills. Live observations may include a range of supervisor interjection in the session—from no interjection to the supervisor extensively supporting skill development in the moment. Recording consultations has an advantage over live observations in that recordings can be reviewed by you and your supervisor multiple times and paused and discussed after the session is complete.

Recordings and observations are combined with review of the session by you and your supervisors (e.g., watching the video); your transcription of part or all of the consultation session; directed self-reflection on your own skill development (see Appendix B for a process log format); supervisor written feedback on your reflections and transcription; and discussion in supervision, with explicit reference to observed behaviors and reflections (see Newman, 2012, for a full description of this process). An example of how you can analyze a transcript or portion of a transcript is the use of the left side/right side procedure, demonstrated in Activity 10.1, along with some questions for you to address. Table 10.1 provides a set of reflective analysis questions. Two additional models for analyzing recordings, adapted here from the psychotherapy supervision literature (Gonsalvez, Brockman, & Hill, 2016) for supervision of school consultation, are delineated in Tables 10.2 and 10.3. Each of these techniques can be flexibly applied to work best for the supervisor and CIT. For example, the five points highlighted in the Give-Me-5 technique could focus on five CIT strengths and needs; five critical incidences; five session themes; five specific consultation skills; or another area relevant to CIT development.

ACTIVITY 10.1 (INDIVIDUAL, GROUP)

Left–Right Reflection Format

Here is a format to support your analysis of a consultation session transcript. On the analysis side, it is useful to reflect on your understanding of what the consultee stated, as well as what you said as a consultant. You can also use the analysis column to practice providing alternative consultant-in-training (CIT) responses that might have been helpful.

We have provided a model of one CIT's use of this format, but would like to encourage you to add to the analysis by providing alternative responses that might have been helpful at different points in the session.

Question for Reflection:

1. What might the CIT have actually said to obtain more clarity? Write your alternative CIT response in the analysis column.

Transcript	Analysis
CIT: Have you gathered any information?	
TC: When the reading analysis was done In September, he had 94 miscues, which is not like 94%. If your word recognition is 94, that is significant. His comprehension was like a 65%, so his comprehension is on a frustration level, and this was a fifth-grade IRI that was given. The fact that he is going back in the text and is still getting 65%, and that is about what I see. I see better word recognition than comprehension, but like I said, I can do another IRI this week.	I'm thinking that I don't fully understand what she is talking about and how I am going to talk to her in reference to this information.
CIT: You said that he appears to be on frustration level with his comprehension. Have you done any reading with something below grade-level?	I jumped on the term frustration level and decided to see if she has worked with him on material that was below frustration level.
TC: Well, the novel he is working on right now, I have two groups, and his is slightly easier than what the other group is doing, and they work in small groups. When he himself is reading independently, we try to make sure it's on— you don't give children frustration level.	
CIT: Okay, so you have been working with him on reading passages that he is not at frustration level with.	Trying to clarify what she just told me.
TC: Well, that is something that is hard to say because of decoding. He can read though but he doesn't necessarily have the comprehension. That is one of the things I'm seeing. It's really hard with Billy to figure out whether he's comprehending or not; he's not clear in his writing, so it's hard to tell if it's his writing or his reading comprehension. I think this time when I give him the IRI, I'll give him one probably start off with fourth-grade and do a series of them and see where he leaves that frustration level.	
CIT: Also, we can take a look at where he is based on your expectations and the curriculum and the instructional level just to make sure if there is a match or anything can be done so that he's not at frustration level, because maybe if he's always at frustration level, then it's not very motivating, because he doesn't know where else to turn.	At this point I don't know where I should go with the information I have already obtained, and I don't know what info I still need, so I became uncomfortable and started rambling.
TC: Yeah, I mean I'll do the IRI to find out according to that what level he's on. Um, we do what we can, I just don't want you to think I give him work all the time that's at that level.	Case in point that rambling gets you into trouble. I wanted to disappear after she said this.
CIT: Oh no, I don't!	

TABLE 10.1 Reflective Analysis Questions

1. What were essential strengths of your behavior during the session?
2. What, if anything, would you change about your behavior during the session?
3. Do you think the session was successful? Why?
4. Which specific factors were important to the outcome?
5. What, if any, unanticipated outcomes resulted from the session?
6. Can you think of alternative approaches to your consultation goals that might have led to a better process?
7. Do you think the content covered was important to the teacher? Why?
8. Did any moral or ethical concerns occur as a result of the session?

TABLE 10.2 The Give-Me-5 Technique for Video Review and Feedback in Consultation Supervision

Step	Description
1	• The CIT records a consultation session and selects an uninterrupted excerpt that best captures the meeting
2	• The CIT reviews the recording and composes notes with three columns: time, observation, and inferences/conclusions
	• The CIT writes down a summary of five key points from the session to discuss with the supervisor
3	• The CIT and supervisor review the recording together within a supervision meeting
	• The supervisor writes down a summary of five key points from the session to discuss with the CIT
4	• The CIT and supervisor compare and discuss their notes and five key points
5	• If applicable, roleplaying is used to support consultation skill development
6	• The supervisor summarizes observations and implications
	• The supervisor and CIT debrief
	• If applicable, next steps for consultation and supervision are determined

Note: CIT = consultant-in-training.

Evaluating Consultation Outcomes

In addition, the effectiveness of the consultation itself can be assessed. This may include a combination of measures: consultee and client change, adherence to the consultation model/process, social validity of interventions, and whether the consultee applies new skills learned during the consultation in future problem-solving efforts (Kaiser, Rosenfield, & Gravois, 2009). Based on 274 teachers in six school districts, Kaiser et al. (2009) documented a number of consultee outcomes, including satisfaction with the consultation experience, confidence about handling similar problems in the future, and learning skills that would be useful in addressing similar concerns. Their findings showed congruence between the teacher perceptions and student outcomes in a subset of cases. They have also provided an example of a teacher survey that could be used with individual teachers or at the school level to assess consultee outcomes. Focusing on a single domain,

TABLE 10.3 The I-Spy Technique for Video Review and Feedback in Consultation Supervision

Step	Description
1	• The supervisor and CIT identify a microskill (e.g., a communication skill) to target for change
2	• The CIT records a consultation session and selects an uninterrupted excerpt that best captures the meeting
	• The CIT reviews the recording in search of applications of the microskill
	• Occurrences are tagged (e.g., 3 min, 30 sec) and alternative responses, as appropriate, are proposed
3	• The CIT and supervisor review the recording together
	• The supervisor searches for additional opportunities of microskill application and/or alternative responses
4	• If applicable, roleplaying is used to support consultation skill development
5	• The supervisor summarizes observations and implications
	• The supervisor and CIT debrief
	• If applicable, next steps for consultation and supervision are determined

Note: CIT = consultant-in-training.

such as client outcomes alone, does not provide sufficient data for evaluating the development of consultation competency.

Client outcomes are also important, although consultants may have less control over that, given consultees usually control intervention implementation and implementation integrity. The IC model has consistently used the Student Documentation Form (SDF) data to evaluate whether consultation goals for the student clients have been met, including goal attainment data, effect on special education placements, and results with students of color (see, e.g., Rosenfield et al., 2014). Data collected to evaluate progress can be helpful to CITs in evaluating client outcomes.

A multi-dimensional evaluation process of consultation competency development can be developed together with your supervisor.

Who Evaluates?

Several individuals may contribute to evaluations of competency development, including self, field supervisors, university supervisors, peers, consultees, and clients. Gathering information from a number of sources on a number of points of interest allows for data triangulation and bias reduction within the supervision evaluation process (Kaslow et al., 2009).

Self-assessment is a critical skill throughout psychologists' careers and can provide an excellent starting point for supervisor–supervisee interactions. Of course, self-assessments are inherently subjective, and you may inadvertently underestimate or overestimate your skills, or simply not know what you do not know. Some supervisees may be dishonest in their self-assessments due to fear of repercussions in supervision. Therefore, self-assessments are best compared with supervisor assessments (field and/or university) completed on the same scale. Discussions of these data can inform goals for your consultation training and directions for future supervision. Peers can also evaluate and provide feedback to one another, for example through observing each other in course simulations or live consultations during field-based experiences and engaging in peer supervision.

Consultees might provide ratings about your work, which offers information on how the consultation was received. Though such ratings attempt to measure social validity, some consultees may be concerned about you receiving a poor grade for your consultation assignment and therefore might rate the consultation as more helpful than they actually perceived it to be (Guiney & Zilbulsky, 2016). Clients may also provide feedback about the consultation. However, since consultation is an indirect service, the feedback would focus primarily on problem improvement based on implemented interventions, which may not directly reflect your work.

Feedback

Evaluation data should be linked to systematic, ongoing, and formal feedback from a knowledgeable other; this is the second leg of the consultation competency development process. Feedback should be timely, frequent, objective, consistent, clear, specific, credible, balanced, collaborative, and occur within the context of a strong supervisory relationship (Heckman-Stone, 2003). Ideally, feedback is also bidirectional, so you will have a chance to report to your supervisors on your perceptions of what is and is not working well in the supervision process (APA, 2015). For example, a supervisor might ask supervisees "what would be helpful for us to do in this supervision meeting?" at the beginning of supervision meetings, and check in midway and at the end of meetings by asking if we are accomplishing what we set out to do. In our experience, this has resulted in supervisees requesting further clarification on points that are unclear, and us providing additional strategies (e.g., modeling how to say something in the consultation session) that we didn't initially recognize were needed by the supervisee.

Just as evaluating process skills is challenging, it can be challenging for supervisors to provide feedback on such skills and for supervisees to receive this feedback. For example, imagine you are a supervisee receiving the following feedback in supervision. Which of these would be easier for you to hear and to try and improve upon?

> **Supervisor:** "I am wondering if the consultation relationship is evolving collaboratively. It seems you have taken over responsibility for the intervention and that you may have left the consultee behind."

> **Supervisor:** "It sounds like the intervention may be missing some components that would help it work more effectively. This may need to be revisited with the consultee."

As demonstrated in the first statement, getting feedback on process skills is almost always *personal*; it can be challenging to accept, let alone to address in practice. On the other hand, feedback on content such as intervention design, implementation, or evaluation is easier to accept and to immediately address. Therefore, process skill feedback is best tied to behaviorally anchored data as captured through observation, transcription, and supervisee self-reflection.

Table 10.4 highlights several examples of concerns that might present themselves during CITs' early consultation interactions. Such concerns can be subtle but require immediate feedback from a consultation supervisor in support of the CIT's improved professional behaviors. Although *working on the process* is in many ways challenging, it is a critical growth avenue for consultees (Newman, 2012).

You, as a supervisee, can be an active guide (versus passive recipient) in the supervision feedback process by identifying areas in which you perceive the need for additional support. You and your supervisors can also preemptively consider frequently occurring concerns faced by novice consultants, discuss strategies to overcome barriers, and recognize that many concerns you are experiencing are typical for new consultants. For example, Newman (2012) and Cramer and Rosenfield (2004) provided multiple examples of common CIT concerns, including becoming fluent in the problem-solving process, using data, communicating systematically, building

TABLE 10.4 Professional Behavior Concerns That May Manifest During Consultation Communication Interactions and Require Supervisor Feedback

Professional Behaviors	
Verbal	*Non-Verbal*
• Talks as a "layperson" rather than as a professional (e.g., use of "like," "um," or other filler language)	• Dresses unprofessionally
• Relationship becomes too friendly, preventing professional work (e.g., excessive storytelling or talking about personal lives instead of the problem)	• Physical proximity to consultee is too close or too distant when speaking
• Uses excessive jargon	• Avoids making eye-contact
• Asks questions without seeming to listen to responses by pausing, paraphrasing, or summarizing	• Is over-reliant on supporting materials (e.g., problem-solving checklist)
• Ignores or glosses over consultee frustration, emotional expression, or need for ventilation	• Nods head, even when disagrees with what the consultee is saying
• De-emphasizes collaboration (e.g., "I can…," rather than, "We can…")	• Appears closed-off or disinterested in conversation
• Talks too quickly or too much	• Default face is dissonant with what is happening (e.g., "thinking face" looks bored or angry)
• Asks double-barreled or vague questions	• Appears outwardly nervous or is paralyzed by nerves
• Engages in advice-giving before the problem is clear	• Is unprepared for consultation meetings

relationships, and bridging paradigm differences between training program views of consultation and the enactment of the consultant role in the field. More recently, Hatzichristou, Lampropoulou, Georgouleas, and Mihou (2017) reported that Greek consultation students found many of the same difficulties as those in the US.

Deliberate Practice

The final leg of the stool supporting the development of school consultation competence is deliberate practice (DP). DP is defined as mindful and systematic practice that occurs over time and requires a knowledgeable other (e.g., a supervisor or mentor) to support the learning process via direct instruction, observation, and feedback (Ericsson & Pool, 2016). Several hallmarks of DP put forth by Ericsson and Pool (2016) also apply to DP of school consultation:

- Includes pre-established training techniques overseen by a supervisor.
- Takes place outside of the trainee's comfort zone.
- Is goal-oriented, including short-term and long-term goals.
- Is deliberate, requiring full attention from the consultant trainee.
- Is combined with feedback from a supervisor (or mentor, or teacher).
- Produces and depends on improved mental representations (i.e., structures allowing us to recognize and remember patterns) of trainee performance.
- Involves continuous improvement upon previously acquired skills.

DP is hard work and is not necessarily "enjoyable," especially at first. One of us (SR) is experiencing that feeling as she learns Tai Chi, where novices are told that it takes months to learn, months to become comfortable, and a lifetime to develop expertise. As Ericsson and Pool (2016) state:

> It's hard to keep going, and even if you keep up your training—you go to the gym regularly, or you practice the guitar for a certain number of hours every week—it's hard to maintain focus and effort, so you may eventually stop pushing yourself and stop improving.
>
> *(p. 167)*

Indeed, it is way easier to engage in routine, "on-the-fly" consultation than engage in a process of deliberate learning and practice. However, consistent with our initial premise in Chapter 1, we believe consultation is worth the effort to teach, supervise, learn, and practice, given the potential benefits that result for consultants, consultees, clients, and systems.

Consultation Research

In this text we have incorporated the underlying research to the extent possible. However, research in school consultation is ongoing, and there are additional resources of which you should be aware. Two journals that publish school consultation research are: *Journal of Educational and Psychological Consultation*, and the APA Division 13 (Society of Consulting Psychology) journal, *Consulting Psychology Journal: Practice and Research*. In addition, much contemporary research in consultation can be found in the chapters of the *Handbook of Research in School Consultation* (2nd ed.; Erchul & Sheridan, 2014).

There is also a case to be made for practitioners engaging in research. Truscott, Kearney, Matthews, and Daniel (2017) discuss opportunities and methods for practitioners to conduct consultation projects as publishable research, encouraging colleagues to present and publish their work on school-based projects as a contribution to the literature. They provide resources and suggestions for conducting such work. They cite earlier authors, such as Stoner and Green (1992), who recommend conducting school-based projects as local experiments, beginning with scientific basis for the consulting process and interventions, adapting the evidence to the local condition and context, and using scientific methods to evaluate results. Ideas for publishing their results are also provided.

Dr. David Shriberg, editor of the *Journal of Educational and Psychological Consultation*, discusses research in consultation in Video 10.1.

Continuing to Build Your Competence

Consistent with competency in any domain area, building competence in school consultation requires the development of particular knowledge, skills, and values. But it requires personal commitment, as in the Tai Chi saying: "As your intention, so shall it be." In this book, we have provided a starting point for your development in each of these areas, which we hope will inspire you to continue your development.

Dr. Markeda Newell discusses the development of school consultation competency in Video 10.2.

Knowledge

Competent consultants possess a clear guiding framework that informs their consultation practice. The School Consultation (SC) model articulated throughout the text is built on research-based features developed from several consultation models and is aligned with the needs of teachers and students in contemporary school settings. We hope you find this framework to be a meaningful and pragmatic guide to your consultation work. Knowledge of culture, relationship-building, communication skills, and the problem-solving stages, and their features, are core to the model. We have offered you detailed nuts and bolts components of the stages and described nuances in their implementation to help you navigate. However, as you have hopefully gleaned from reading the book, the SC model is more than a series of problem-solving stages. The model is situated within a school context and therefore requires you to be knowledgeable about school culture, including *why* the norms and regularities in your school are relevant when initiating and conducting consultation services, and *how* best to work in your specific setting. Knowledge of schools as organizational systems, and the role of instructional match in assessing and intervening on problems, are also critical.

Skills

Competent consultants are more than intervention dispensers. Competent consultants are skilled in the nuanced processes of consultation, including building strong relationships with diverse consultees and consultee systems through thoughtful, purposeful communication. Competent consultants are humble consultants who engage in asking before telling and are genuinely interested in understanding the difficulties faced by consultees and supporting changes in the consultees' knowledge, skills, confidence, or objectivity that can ultimately support students. And competent consultants treat consultation as an ongoing process rather than a short-term event; even when the problem is solved, the door remains open for future consultation. In short, being knowledgeable about problem-solving interventions is not enough to be a competent consultant; the skilled application of consultation is also necessary.

Values

We have discussed throughout this book, in some ways explicitly and others implicitly, the values of competent consultants. Competent consultants are ethical consultants, including navigating the intersection of ethics and the consultation relationships (e.g., competence, informed consent, confidentiality, and multiple relationships), and organizational consultation issues (e.g., conflicts of interest, failure to use research science and evidence-based practices, conflicts between organizational demands and ethical practice).

Competent school consultants are also reflective practitioners. Reflection is at the heart of consultation training. The combination of *learning* (e.g., formal coursework, reading), *doing* (e.g., simulated experiences, systematic consultation cases during a practicum or internship), and *reflecting* (e.g., written reflection, recording and reviewing your work) augments the development of consultation competence. Video recording and review, both individually and with a supervisor, are critical components of consultation training. Indeed, this is now standard practice in training of related clinical skills such as counseling (Goodyear et al., 2016). Once you enter the profession, reflection continues with ongoing consideration of your consultation work and how your actions impact consultees, clients/students, and systems.

Danny Newman, co-author, concludes this discussion of building your future competence in Video 10.3.

We hope your developmental journey as a school consultant does not end with your graduate training or upon reading this book. Indeed, several of the video speakers spoke to the continuing process of learning to be a consultant. To consider your own learning process as a consultant thus far and your starting point for future learning, complete Activity 10.2. Examples of how you might forge a path beyond consultation competence, towards consultation expertise, are provided in Table 10.5.

TABLE 10.5 Examples of Actions to Continue Your Professional Learning Focused on School Consultation

Actions

- Seek out additional readings about school consultation, such as some of the materials referenced throughout this book
- Attend presentations focused on school consultation at professional conferences
- Get involved in professional organizations/groups focused on consultation, such as the Society for Consulting Psychology/Division 13 of APA, or NASP's consultee-centered consultation special interest group. Consider becoming a member, attending a conference or meeting, or taking on a leadership role
- Engage in ongoing formative self-assessment regarding your consultation knowledge and skills using one or more of the tools provided in this book, and set professional goals based on current performance
- Seek feedback on your consultation work from a coach, mentor, or supervisor on your consultation skills. If possible, have the coach, mentor, or supervisor directly observe your work through live observation or audio or video recording rather than relying solely on self-report

(continued)

TABLE 10.5 Continued

Actions

- Coordinate a process of peer support, such as a peer supervision group of professionals in your work setting. If possible, have a peer observe your work through live observation or audio or video recording rather than relying solely on self-report
- Become an assistant to the consultation course instructor to supervise and receive supervision on your work
- Engage in applied school consultation research

Note: APA = American Psychological Association. NASP = National Association of School Psychologists.

ACTIVITY 10.2 (INDIVIDUAL)

Revisiting Your Consultation Map

At the beginning of this book (Chapter 1), you wrote down your initial thoughts about school consultation, designed a map to diagram your understanding of school consultation at that point in time, and wrote a brief written summary of your map.

Without looking at your first map, design a new map diagramming your *current* understanding of school consultation. Underneath the map, write a brief written summary of your map.

Questions for Reflection:

1. After completing your new diagram, compare it to your diagram from Chapter 1. How do the diagrams compare to each other?
2. What are the similarities and differences in the diagram? What do these suggest about your learning?
3. Which areas that are in your diagram do you believe require additional training and practice to build competency in consultation?
4. What actions do you need to take to continue to build your own competency as a consultant?

Finally, and perhaps most importantly, competent school consultants value the promise of consultative service delivery. Although this might seem obvious, it is easy for school consultants to get wrapped up in delivering other practices, many of which are interpersonally and professionally isolating, and perhaps less effectual forms of helping. Nearly every aspect of working in schools involves interacting with adults on behalf of students (Gutkin & Conoley, 1990). Consultation should be viewed as a tool to give expertise away to teachers, parents, and others. In turn, through the provision of indirect services, school consultants are able to build, support, and enhance the capacity of the school system, its students, and their families.

APPENDIX A

Assessment of School Climate for Collaboration (Vu et al., 2013)

Please mark the extent to which you agree or disagree with the following:

	Strongly Disagree	Disagree	Neutral	Agree	Strongly Agree
In our school, teachers are expected to work with specialists and other teachers to resolve problems.					
In our school, teachers formally schedule time to collaborate about teaching and learning practices.					
Specialists (e.g., ESOL teachers, special educators, reading teachers) and classroom teachers plan together for students they teach in common.					
Teachers are on their own to solve classroom problems in this school.					
In this school, it is seen as a sign of weakness if a teacher asks for help.					
Teachers are uncomfortable asking for help when they have a behavior problem in their classroom.					
Teachers in this school work together to design instruction.					
Teachers in this school coordinate instructional goals across grade levels.					

	Strongly Disagree	Disagree	Neutral	Agree	Strongly Agree
Teachers in this school consult with each other to improve their own classroom management.					
I am more likely to ask a colleague to work with me on my instruction than to ask them to work with the student.					

APPENDIX B

School Consultation Process Log

Consultant Name: _____

Grade Level of Case: _____

Session Date: _____

1. **Consultation problem-solving stage.**
   a. List what stage of the problem-solving process you are currently engaged in (i.e., Contracting; Problem Identification/Problem Analysis; Intervention Planning; Intervention Implementation, Progress Monitoring, and Performance Feedback; Post-Intervention Planning and Closure).
   b. What components of this stage have you completed thus far?
   c. What components of this stage remain to be completed?
2. **Consultant-consultee working relationship.**
   a. What is the collaborative working dynamic you are experiencing in your case? Embed transcribed excerpts to demonstrate your assessment of collaboration and describe what is demonstrated by the assessment.
3. **Communication skills.**
   a. Reflect on your use of communication/language within the consultation session, including specific skills such as clarifications, paraphrases, perception checking, and summarizing. Embed transcribed excerpts to demonstrate your points.
      i. What communication strategies were successful?
      ii. What could you have done or said differently?
4. **Request(s) for feedback during supervision.**
   a. What are your next steps in the case and the problem-solving process?
   b. What would you like to discuss further in supervision? As possible, try to answer your own questions in this section of the log. Your initial thoughts should be considered in collaboration with a supervisor.

APPENDIX C

Adherence to the School Consultation Process

Please indicate which stage(s) of consultation were observed in the video by indicating the components completed within the stages covered.

Consultant Name: _____ **Date of Consultation Session:** _____
Was a problem-solving stage a continuation from a previous meeting?
(Circle Yes or No)
Which stage(s) was/were continued? _____
Name of Observer: _____ **Date of Observation:** _____

Contracting Stage	*Was Item Completed?*		
Discussed consultee's expectations and prior experiences consulting	Yes	No	Unsure
Introduced the school consultation assumptions, expectations, and process	Yes	No	Unsure
Explained stage-based problem-solving process	Yes	No	Unsure
Clarified school as the context for problem-solving, including the concept of instructional match	Yes	No	Unsure
Explained potential application of problem-solving at multiple tiers in addition to individual students	Yes	No	Unsure
Clarified shared ownership of the problem and the consultation process	Yes	No	Unsure
Clarified non-evaluative nature of the consultation process	Yes	No	Unsure
Explained the parameters of confidentiality	Yes	No	Unsure
Checked for consultee agreement and commitment to participate	Yes	No	Unsure
Scheduled follow-up meeting/ongoing schedule	Yes	No	Unsure

Problem Identification and Problem Analysis	Was Item Completed?		
Created shared understanding of consultee's concern(s) using collaborative communication skills	Yes	No	Unsure
Defined concern(s) in observable terms	Yes	No	Unsure
Defined concern in the context of the school/classroom, and considered the role of instructional match/mismatch	Yes	No	Unsure
Followed up with additional data collection, such as record or work sample review, observation, or instructional assessment	Yes	No	Unsure
Prioritized concerns	Yes	No	Unsure
Established a plan to measure current performance (i.e., baseline)	Yes	No	Unsure
Established baseline measurement of performance	Yes	No	Unsure
Set performance goals based on baseline data	Yes	No	Unsure

Intervention Planning	Was Item Completed?		
Elicited consultee's ideas/strategies	Yes	No	Unsure
Discussed *all* of these: *What* classroom-based strategy will meet goals? *Where* will strategy be implemented? *When* can strategy be implemented? *How often* will strategy be implemented? *Who* will be responsible?	Yes	No	Unsure
Considered conditions to create/maintain instructional match	Yes	No	Unsure
Considered whether multiple students can benefit from the intervention	Yes	No	Unsure
Documented specifics of what, when, how often, and who	Yes	No	Unsure

Intervention Implementation, Monitoring, and Performance Feedback	Was Item Completed?		
Continued meeting while intervention is being implemented	Yes	No	Unsure
Clarified what's working and what needs refining	Yes	No	Unsure
Elicited consultee's perception of progress	Yes	No	Unsure
Provided performance feedback regarding level of adherence to intervention, with consideration given to implementation changes as needed	Yes	No	Unsure
Collaboratively reviewed and discussed data	Yes	No	Unsure
Compared progress with goals	Yes	No	Unsure

Post-Intervention Planning and Closure	Was Item Completed?		
Assessed *all* of these: (a) goals are met; (b) consultee can implement independently if needed; (c) strategies are fading/faded	Yes	No	Unsure
Elicited consultee's plans to maintain student progress	Yes	No	Unsure
Determined documentation of efforts	Yes	No	Unsure
Considered addressing other priority areas not yet addressed	Yes	No	Unsure
If case is explicitly closed, let consultee know how support can be accessed in the future	Yes	No	Unsure
Discussed further communication with parents, colleagues, and teams	Yes	No	Unsure

APPENDIX D

Forms

Instructional Consultation Student Documentation Form

Student's Name_____ Grade_____ Date of Birth_____ Date Started_____
Teacher's Name_____ Case Manager_____ School_____

Goal Attainment Scale (GAS)

Step 1: Initial description of concern				
Step 2: Prioritize	Importance **1 2 3 4** (student at instructional level? Y N)	Importance **1 2 3 4** (student at instructional level? Y N)	Importance **1 2 3 4** (student at instructional level? Y N)	Importance **1 2 3 4** (student at instructional level? Y N)
Step 3: Observable/measurable statement of current performance (following baseline)	Date collected_____	Date collected_____	Date collected_____	Date collected_____
Step 4: Short-term goal: Expected performance in____weeks (4–6 weeks)	Date consistently attained_____	Date consistently attained_____	Date consistently attained_____	Date consistently attained_____
Step 5: Interim goal: Expected behavior in_____ weeks	Date consistently attained_____	Date consistently attained_____	Date consistently attained_____	Date consistently attained_____
Step 6: Long-term goal: Expected behavior in_____ weeks	Date consistently attained_____	Date consistently attained_____	Date consistently attained_____	Date consistently attained_____

Operational Definition of Academic/Behavioral Performance:

Priority #_____
on GAS

KEY
☐ _____
☐ _____
☐ _____

What specific academic/behaviours will be recorded? _____

When will the behavior be recorded? _____
Where will the behavior be recorded? _____

Baseline (Step 3)

End Baseline

Describe intervention design and materials	When and how often?	Persons responsible	Motivational strategies?

Date	Summary of Meetings	Follow-up Activities	Next Meeting Date and Time

APPENDIX E

Intervention Script and Adherence Checklist for Responding to Refusal Behavior

Adapted from Smith, J. (2017). *The use of brief functional analysis to reduce refusal behavior in a first-grade student with an autism spectrum disorder.* (Unpublished second year professional practice portfolio). University of Cincinnati, Cincinnati, OH.

Materials:

- Token Board with numbers
- X tokens

Intervention Script:

1. At the start of a refusal (see operational definition at end of script), provide Jack with two prompts (can include verbal, physical, or gestural prompts) to comply with original instruction.
2. If after two prompts, Jack has not complied with the original instruction, place an X token over the number 1 box and tell Jack, "You earned an X for not listening. Two more Xs, you will have a timeout."
3. After giving the first X, instruct Jack to complete the original instruction. If he begins to refuse again, follow steps 1–3.
4. Once Jack has received 3 Xs, tell him, "It's time for a timeout. Sit in the hallway."
5. Prompt Jack to sit outside the workroom (close the door behind you).
6. Show Jack a visual timer of 1 minute. If he is calm after 1 minute, tell him it is time to work, and go back to the original task.
7. If Jack's behavior escalates and he attempts to run or becomes aggressive, go to the safe room and follow timeout procedures in there.

8. If in the safe room, show Jack a visual timer through the window for 1 minute. If he is calm, go back to the workroom and have him complete the original task.

9. Add 1-minute intervals to his timer as necessary until he is calm. Timeouts should be in a room or area with no or very few items, such as the safe room or the room next to the safe room, when possible. For instance, the sensory room cannot be considered a timeout location because Jack likes to go in there to play and it has preferred items in it.

10. Jack may not have access to any preferred items at this time, which includes Mickey Mouse Doll, Chewy, Kindle, Blanket, Pillow, Lights off, Adult Attention, or any other preferred items. All items should be taken away at this time, including papers or objects that he attempts to take out of the workroom with him.

11. Once Jack has calmed down (stopped crying, yelling, kicking, hitting, etc.), tell Jack, "Thank you for calming down. It's time to finish your work; let's go back."

12. Instruct Jack to complete the original task that caused his refusal behavior. Once he completes task, place the correct number on his choice token board.

13. If Jack begins to refuse again, complete steps 1–12 until he has complied with the task.

Operational Definition of Refusal Behaviors:

Refusals (R): Any instance of student crying for longer than 10 seconds, pushing adult or objects with hands or feet, kicking adult or objects with feet, hitting adult or object with an open hand or a closed fist, grabbing items he is not supposed to have, throwing items, yelling for longer than 10 seconds, screaming for longer than 10 seconds, running/walking away from task or assigned area, or falling to the floor when given a directive or a demand has been placed on him.

Examples of Refusal Behavior:

- Teacher instructs student to begin work time. Student pushes items off the table and crawls under the table.
- Teacher and student are walking in the hallway. Student sees an instrument in the hallway. Student grabs instrument. Teacher tells student, "no," and takes the instrument from student. Student pushes teacher and hits teacher to get the instrument back.
- Teacher tells student it is time to go to gym. Student points to sensory room. Teacher tells student: "gym first, then sensory room." Student runs towards the door. Teacher blocks door. Student hits, kicks, and pushes in an attempt to get out of the door.

Data collection plan to monitor progress:

University of Cincinnati school psychology practicum students will observe the 2:00 PM to 2:30 PM work time 2× per week. During 10-second intervals, compliance will be recorded using momentary time sampling, and refusals will be recorded using partial interval recording.

Adherence checks will consist of the two practicum students completing a checklist on the steps followed in the intervention script 1x per week.

Adherence Check for Jack's Intervention

Name of Teacher:

Date:

1. _____ Before beginning the session, Mickey Mouse Doll is placed out of reach
2. _____ Student is asked to choose reinforcement from his choice board
3. _____ Student places reinforcement token on his token board
4. _____ Teacher prompts student to complete activity 1 and places the number 1 on the token board
5. _____ Teacher prompts student to complete activity 2 and places the number 2 on the token board
6. _____ Teacher prompts student to complete activity 3 and places the number 3 on the token board
7. _____ Teacher prompts student to complete activity 4 and places the number 4 on the token board (this activity can be student's choice or the teacher's choice)
8. _____ Teacher provides praise throughout the session
9. _____ Teacher provides redirection as-needed to stay on task
10. _____ Teacher provides student with chosen reinforcement as soon as the 4th token is earned

Total Checked _____

Total Available _____

Adherence % (Total Checked/Total Available) _____

Adherence Check for Jack's Timeouts

Name of Teacher:

Date:

1. When a refusal occurs:

_____ Provides student 2 prompts to comply with original instruction

_____ Places X token over number box if student does not comply with original instructions, and explains why the X was placed

_____ Instructs student to complete original instructions

2. When the student receives 3 Xs:

_____ Tells him that it is time for a timeout and to sit in the hallway

_____ Prompts him to sit outside the workroom

_____ Sets and shows him a visual timer of 1 minute If student is calm after 1 minute:

_____ Goes back into workroom and instructs him to complete the original task

If student is *not* calm after 1 minute:

_____ Takes him to safe room

3. When student is in safe room:

_____ Does not let him have access to any preferred items

_____ Shows him a visual timer of 1 minute through the window

If student is calm after 1 minute:

_____ Takes him back to the workroom and instructs him to complete the original task

If student is *not* calm after 1 minute:

_____ Adds 1-minute intervals to timer until he is calm

Once calm:

_____ Thanks him for calming down and tells him that is time to finish his work

_____ Takes him back to the workroom and instructs him to complete the original task

Total Checked _____

Total Available _____

Adherence % (Total Checked/Total Available) _____

APPENDIX F

Self-Assessment of Consultation Competence

From Burkhouse, K. S. (2012). Educating a reflective school consultant: Multi-faceted techniques. In S. Rosenfield (Ed.). *Becoming a school consultant: Lessons learned*. New York: Routledge.

Name: Date: Circle one: PRE MID POST RETRO-PRE

NA = No prior knowledge or skill in this area
AW = Awareness: able to generally articulate concept
CU = Conceptual Understanding: able to clearly articulate concept and describe appropriate actions
SA = Skill Acquisition: able to demonstrate skill or knowledge in structured or simulated settings
AP = Application of Skills: able to use skill or knowledge flexibly in actual setting

Consultation Skill Area	NA	AW	CU	SA	AP
Collaboration and Consultative Skills					
Form working relationships with diverse consultees					
Understand consultee's strengths and needs					
Flexibly adhere to problem-solving process					
Successfully address difficulties that arise in consultation					
Use Student Documentation Form (SDF) to facilitate consultation process					
Share problem-solving process with consultee and make joint decisions through the process					
Interpersonal Communication Skills					
Clarify consultee's concerns through use of paraphrasing, summarizing, and asking questions					
Reflect feelings of consultee					

(*continued*)

Adapt communication to meet needs of consultee
Respond to non-verbal cues of consultee
Reflect on thoughts and ideas of consultee
Use clarifying questions appropriately
Acknowledge differences of opinions and resolve conflicts

Problem-Solving Process

Address all areas of contracting
Create a shared understanding of consultee's concerns
Conceptualize consultee's concerns in observable and
measureable terms
Gather data based on curriculum expectations to aid in
problem-solving process
Assess student's instructional match
Conduct Curriculum Based Assessment (CBA) and/or
Instructional Assessment (IA) appropriately in cases
Conduct systematic observations across multiple settings
Prioritize concerns of consultee

Problem-Solving Process Continued

Set measurable goals with consultee
Elicit teacher's ideas for strategies in coordination with
goals
Discuss intervention plans related to EBI
Use instructional match in intervention design and
selection
Incorporate student's or group's prior knowledge into
intervention plan
Select materials to build on student's skills
Anticipate potential barriers to implementation
Evaluate student progress using data
Follow-up and monitor implementation of intervention
plan
Rework conceptualization of problem and intervention
based on data

Professional Interaction Skills

Work through obstacles and difficult issues with supervisor
Focus on best interest of consultee and client
Respect the culture and practices of the school
Interact effectively with school personnel
Consider cultural differences in consultation triad
Recognize, respect, and respond appropriately to the
effects of personal values and belief systems of self and
others in the consultation process
Exhibit caring, respectful, empathic, congruent, and open
consultation interactions
Be willing to admit that you do not know an answer and
willing to explore possible solutions with others

(continued)

Demonstrate willingness to learn from others throughout
consultation experience

Give and solicit feedback to maintain, revise, or terminate
consultation activities

Relate to peers in professional manner

Engage in self-evaluation of strengths and weaknesses
to modify personal behaviors that may influence
consultation process

Demonstrate investment in becoming a skilled consultant

Systems Change

View self as change agent and continue development of
the role of change agent

Conduct system-wide needs assessments

Identify benefits and consequences from proposed change
efforts

Evaluate programs that seek systemic change

APPENDIX G

Consultant Self-Efficacy Scale
(Guiney, Harris, Zusho, & Cancelli, 2014)

Name: _____

Please read each of the following statements carefully and indicate the extent to which you feel confident about what is described. Rate each statement on a scale from 1 (Not At All Confident) to 9 (Extremely Confident).

How confident are you that you...	*1 = Not at all*					*9 = Extremely*			
1. Can remain aware of the potential impact of your personal experiences while consulting	1	2	3	4	5	6	7	8	9
2. Can reflect on your performance after a consultation session has finished	1	2	3	4	5	6	7	8	9
3. Can identify areas for improvement in future consultation sessions after a session has concluded	1	2	3	4	5	6	7	8	9
4. Can critically evaluate the success of a consultation case after it has been terminated	1	2	3	4	5	6	7	8	9
5. Can identify areas for improvement in future consultation cases after a case has been terminated	1	2	3	4	5	6	7	8	9
6. Can establish a strong working relationship with most consultees	1	2	3	4	5	6	7	8	9
7. Can demonstrate non-verbal behaviors that indicate you are attending to your consultee	1	2	3	4	5	6	7	8	9
8. Can establish a working relationship with a consultee who demonstrates resistance to consultation	1	2	3	4	5	6	7	8	9
9. Can establish a working relationship with a consultee who is consulting with you only because it is a prereferral requirement	1	2	3	4	5	6	7	8	9

(continued)

How confident are you that you…	$1 = $ Not at all					$9 = $ Extremely			
10. Can establish a collaborative relationship that respects your consultee's expertise and knowledge	1	2	3	4	5	6	7	8	9
11. Can ask open-ended questions to encourage a consultee to further explore his or her concerns	1	2	3	4	5	6	7	8	9
12. Can frame a consultee's concerns in terms of observable, measurable behaviors	1	2	3	4	5	6	7	8	9
13. Can elicit responses from a consultee that will lead to problem identification	1	2	3	4	5	6	7	8	9
14. Can redirect the focus back to the student when the discussion strays to other topics (such as non-work-related problems)	1	2	3	4	5	6	7	8	9
15. Can successfully use reframing (helping your consultee see the problem from a different perspective)	1	2	3	4	5	6	7	8	9
16. Can restore a consultee's objectivity when necessary or appropriate	1	2	3	4	5	6	7	8	9
17. Can address a lack of confidence when detected in your consultee	1	2	3	4	5	6	7	8	9
18. Can recognize and deal with theme interference or transference from your consultee	1	2	3	4	5	6	7	8	9
19. Can collaborate with a consultee to list potential interventions to address the identified problem	1	2	3	4	5	6	7	8	9
20. Can assist the consultee to select an intervention that will be effective in addressing the client's problem(s)	1	2	3	4	5	6	7	8	9
21. Can plan for the collection of data to monitor the effectiveness of an intervention that is implemented	1	2	3	4	5	6	7	8	9
22. Can help consultees develop data-collection skills so that they will have the ability to make data-driven decisions in the future	1	2	3	4	5	6	7	8	9
23. Can plan for the collection of behavioral data to monitor an intervention	1	2	3	4	5	6	7	8	9
24. Can evaluate the effectiveness of an intervention that is implemented	1	2	3	4	5	6	7	8	9
25. Can work with a consultee to plan ways of generalizing the effects of an intervention beyond the setting in which it is used	1	2	3	4	5	6	7	8	9
26. Can develop means of fading an intervention once it has been successful	1	2	3	4	5	6	7	8	9
27. Have knowledge of evidence-based interventions to address academic difficulties	1	2	3	4	5	6	7	8	9
28. Can find information regarding evidence-based interventions for addressing new or unfamiliar referral problems	1	2	3	4	5	6	7	8	9
29. Can guide the consultation process through stages from contracting through termination	1	2	3	4	5	6	7	8	9

(continued)

How confident are you that you...	1 = Not at all							9 = Extremely

30. Can explain the process of consultation to a new consultee — 1 2 3 4 5 6 7 8 9

31. Can evaluate the consultation experience with a consultee upon termination of a case — 1 2 3 4 5 6 7 8 9

32. Can utilize the process of consultation to address academic difficulties — 1 2 3 4 5 6 7 8 9

33. Can utilize the process of consultation to address social-emotional difficulties — 1 2 3 4 5 6 7 8 9

34. Can implement a behavioral consultation (BC) or problem-solving consultation model when necessary or appropriate — 1 2 3 4 5 6 7 8 9

35. Can implement a mental health consultation model when necessary or appropriate — 1 2 3 4 5 6 7 8 9

36. Can implement a systems-level or organizational consultation model when necessary or appropriate — 1 2 3 4 5 6 7 8 9

37. Can consult with a teacher around a client (student) with ADHD — 1 2 3 4 5 6 7 8 9

38. Can consult with a teacher around a client (student) with a pervasive developmental disorder (PDD) — 1 2 3 4 5 6 7 8 9

39. Can consult with a teacher around a client (student) who is an English language learner (ELL) — 1 2 3 4 5 6 7 8 9

40. Can consult effectively with someone of a cultural background that is different from yours — 1 2 3 4 5 6 7 8 9

41. Can consult effectively with a teacher when the client (student) is from a different cultural background than your own — 1 2 3 4 5 6 7 8 9

42. Can recognize your inherent biases or assumptions about clients and/or consultees based on cultural background — 1 2 3 4 5 6 7 8 9

43. Can remain aware of how your cultural background may affect the assumptions you make about consultees, clients, or consultation cases — 1 2 3 4 5 6 7 8 9

44. Can recognize how your consultee's cultural background may affect the way in which he or she approaches a consultation experience — 1 2 3 4 5 6 7 8 9

45. Can recognize when your personal beliefs are affecting your approach to a consultee or case — 1 2 3 4 5 6 7 8 9

REFERENCES

Alpert, J. L., & Meyers, J. (Eds.). (1983). *Training in consultation: Perspectives from mental health, behavioral, and organizational consultation.* Springfield, IL: C. C. Thomas.

American Psychological Association. (2006). Evidence-based practice in psychology. *American Psychologist, 61,* 271–285.

American Psychological Association. (2015). Guidelines for clinical supervision in health service psychology. *American Psychologist, 70,* 33–46.

American Psychological Association. (2017). *Guidelines for education and training at the doctoral and postdoctoral level in consulting psychology (CP)/organizational consulting psychology.* Retrieved from http://preview.apa.org/about/policy/education-training.pdf

Anderson, H., & Goolishian, H. A. (1988). Human systems as linguistic systems: Preliminary and evolving ideas about the implications for clinical theory. *Family Process, 27,* 371–393.

Anton-LaHart, J., & Rosenfield, S. (2004). A survey of preservice consultation training in school psychology programs. *Journal of Educational and Psychological Consultation, 15,* 41–62.

Archer, A. L., & Hughes, C. A. (2011). *Explicit instruction: Effective and efficient teaching.* New York: Guilford Press.

Argyris, C., Putnam, R., & Smith, D. M. (1985). *Action science: Concepts, methods, and skills for research and intervention.* San Francisco: Jossey-Bass.

Bailey, J. S., & Burch, M. R. (2017). *Research methods in applied behavior analysis.* New York: Routledge.

Barrett, C. A. (2012). Making the instructional match salient for the teacher. In S. A. Rosenfield (Ed.), *Becoming a school consultant: Lessons learned* (pp. 127–138). New York: Routledge.

Barrett, C. A., Newman, D. S., & Hazel, C. E. (2018, February). *Systems-level consultation: Expanding your role for the benefit of all.* Accepted mini-skills workshop presented at the annual convention of the National Association of School Psychologists, Chicago, IL.

Batsche, G., Elliott, J., Graden, J., Grimes, J., Kovaleski, J., Prasse, D., Reschley, D., Schrag, J., …, & Tilly, D. (2005). *Response to intervention: Policy considerations and implementation.* Alexandria, VA: National Association of State Directors of Special Education.

Belar, C. D. (2009). Advancing the culture of competence. *Training and Education in Professional Psychology, 3*, S63–S65.

Benishek, L. E., Gregory, M. E., Hodges, K., Newell, M., Hughes, A. M., Marlow, S., Lacerenza, C., Rosenfield, S., & Salas, E. (2016). Bringing the science of team training to school-based teams. *Theory Into Practice, 55*, 111–118.

Benn, A. L. (2004). Communities of practice: Study of one school's first year of implementation of a new problem-solving model (Unpublished doctoral dissertation). University of Maryland, College Park, MD.

Bergan, J. R. (1977). *Behavioral consultation*. Columbus, OH: Charles E. Merrill.

Bergan, J. R., & Kratochwill, T. R. (1990). *Applied clinical psychology: Behavioral consultation and therapy*. New York: Plenum Press.

Berger, J. (2012). Who owns the classroom homework problem? In S. A. Rosenfield (Ed.), *Becoming a school consultant: Lessons learned* (pp. 163–176). New York: Routledge.

Berger, W. (2014). *A more beautiful question: The power of inquiry to spark breakthrough ideas*. New York: Bloomsbury.

Bersoff, D. N., & Grieger, R. I. (1971). An interview model for the psychosituational assessment of children's behavior. *American Journal of Orthopsychiatry, 41*, 483–493.

Bloom, B. S. (1976). *Human characteristics and school learning*. New York: McGraw-Hill.

Borgelt, C., & Conoley, J. C. (1999). Psychology in the schools: Systems intervention case examples. In C. R. Reynolds & T. B. Gutkin (Eds.), *The handbook of school psychology* (3rd ed., pp. 1056–1076). New York: Wiley.

Burkhouse, K. S. (2012). Educating a reflective school consultant: Multi-faceted techniques. In S. A. Rosenfield (Ed.), *Becoming a school consultant: Lessons learned* (pp. 25–47). New York: Routledge.

Burns, M. K., Jimerson, S. R., VanDerHeyden, A. M., & Deno, S. L. (2016). Toward a unified response-to-intervention model: Multi-tiered systems of support. In Jimerson, S. R., Burns, M. K., & VanDerHeyden, A. M. (Eds.), *Handbook of response to intervention* (pp. 719–732). Boston, MA: Springer .

Burns, M. K., & Parker, D. C. (2014). *Curriculum-based assessment for instructional design: Using data to individual instruction*. New York: Guilford.

Camera, L. (2015, September 16). Wanted: Minority teachers. Diversity among teachers in the U.S. hasn't caught up with the large number of minority students. *U.S. News and World Report*. Retrieved from www.usnews.com/news/blogs/data-mine/2015/09/16/teacher-workforce-not-diverse-enough-report-shows

Caplan, G. (1970). *The theory and practice of mental health consultation*. New York: Basic Books.

Carner, L. A. (1982). Developing a consultative contract. In J. L. Alpert (Ed.), *Psychological consultation in educational settings* (pp. 8–32). San Francisco: Jossey-Bass.

Castillo, J. M., Curtis, M. J., & Gelley, C. (2012). School psychology 2010 - part 2: School psychologists' professional practices and implications for the field. *Communique, 40*(8), 4–6.

Chafouleas, S. M., Clonan, S. M., & Vanauken, T. L. (2002). A national survey of current supervision and evaluation practices of school psychologists. *Psychology in the Schools, 39*, 317–325.

Conoley, J. C., & Conoley, C. W. (1992). *School consultation: Practice and training*. New York: Pearson College Division.

Conoley, J. C., & Conoley, C. W. (2010). Why does collaboration work? Linking positive psychology and collaboration. *Journal of Educational and Psychological Consultation, 20*, 75–82.

Cramer, K., & Rosenfield, S. (2004). Clinical supervision of consultation. *The Clinical Supervisor, 22*(1), 111–124.

Curtis, M. J., Castillo, J. M., & Cohen, R. M. (2008). Best practices in system-level change. In A. Thomas & J. Grimes (Eds.), *Best practices in school psychology V* (pp. 887–902). Bethesda, MD: NASP.

Daly, E. J. III, Doll, B., Schulte, A. C., & Fenning, P. (2011). The competencies initiative in American professional psychology: Implications for school psychology preparation. *Psychology in the Schools, 48*, 872–886.

Darling-Hammond, L., Wei, R. C., Andree, A., Richardson, N., & Orphanos, S. (2009). *Professional learning in the learning profession: A status report on teacher development in the United States and abroad.* Dallas, TX: National Staff Development Council.

Dart, E. H., Cook, C. R., Collins, T. A., Gresham, F. M., & Chenier, J. S. (2012). Test driving interventions to increase treatment integrity and student outcomes. *School Psychology Review, 41*, 467–481.

Desimone, L. M., & Garet, M. S. (2015). Best practices in teachers' professional development in the United States. *Psychology, Society and Education, 7*(3), 252–263.

Dillon, J. T. (1979). Defects of questioning as an interview technique. *Psychology in the Schools, 16*, 575–580.

Di Stefano, G., Gino, F., Pisano, G. P., & Staats, B. (2014). *Learning by thinking: How reflection aids performance.* Boston: Harvard Business School.

Doll, B., Haack, K., Kosse, S., Osterloh, M., Siemers, E., & Pray, B. (2005). The dilemma of pragmatics: Why schools don't use quality team consultation practices. *Journal of Educational and Psychological Consultation, 16*, 127–155.

Donohoo, J. (2017). *Collective efficacy: How educators' beliefs impact student learning.* Thousand Oaks, CA: Corwin/Sage.

Dougherty, A. M. (2013). *Psychological consultation and collaboration in school and community settings* (6th ed.). Belmont, CA: Brooks/Cole.

Dougherty, A. M., Tack, F. E., Fullam, C. B., & Hammer, L. A. (1996). Disengagement: A neglected aspect of the consultation process. *Journal of Educational and Psychological Consultation, 7*, 259–274.

Doyle, A. C. (1894). *Round the red lamp: Being facts and fancies of medical life.* New York: D. Appleton.

D'zurilla, T. J., & Goldfried, M. R. (1971). Problem solving and behavior modification. *Journal of Abnormal Psychology, 78*, 107–126.

Embry, D. D., & Biglan, A. (2008). Evidence-based kernels: Fundamental units of behavioral influence. *Clinical Child Family Psychology Review, 11*, 75–113.

Erchul, W. P. (2011). School consultation and response to intervention: A tale of two literatures. *Journal of Educational and Psychological Consultation, 21*, 191–208.

Erchul, W. P., Grissom, P. F., Getty, K. C., & Bennett, M. S. (2014). Researching interpersonal influence within school consultation: Social power base and relational communication perspectives. In W. P. Erchul & S. Sheridan (Eds.), *Handbook of research in school consultation* (2nd ed., pp. 349–385). New York: Routledge.

Erchul, W. P., & Sheridan, S. (Eds.). (2014). *Handbook of research in school consultation* (2nd ed.). New York: Routledge.

Ericsson, A., & Pool, R. (2016). *Peak: Secrets from the new science of expertise.* Boston, MA: Houghton Mifflin Harcourt.

Ericsson, K. A. (Ed.). (2009). *Development of professional expertise: Toward measurement of expert performance and design of optimal learning environments.* New York: Cambridge University Press.

Fallon, L. M., Collier-Meek, M. A., Maggin, D. M., Sanetti, L. M., & Johnson, A. H. (2015). Is performance feedback for educators an evidence-based practice? A systematic review and evaluation based on single-case research. *Exceptional Children, 81*, 227–246.

Farbman, D. A. (2015). *The case for improving and expanding time in school: A review of key research and practice*. Boston, MA: National Center on Time and Learning.

Fenning, P., Diaz, Y., Valley-Gray, S., Cash, R., Spearman, C., Hazel, C. E., Grunewald, S., Riccio, C., & Harris, A. (2015). Perceptions of competencies among school psychology trainers and practitioners: What matters? *Psychology in the Schools, 52*, 1032–1041.

Fouad, N. A., Grus, C. L., Hatcher, R. L., Kaslow, N. J., Hutchings, P. S., Madson, M., Collins, Jr., F. L., & Crossman, R. E. (2009). Competency benchmarks: A model for the understanding and measuring of competence in professional psychology across training levels. *Training and Education in Professional Psychology, 3*, S5–S26.

Fuchs, L. S., & Fuchs, D. (1986). Effects of systematic formative evaluation: A meta-analysis. *Exceptional Children, 53*, 199–208.

Gallessich, J. (1982). *The profession and practice of consultation: A handbook for consultants, trainers of consultants, and consumers of consultation services*. San Francisco: Jossey-Bass.

Garmston, R. J., & Wellman, B. M. (2009). *The adaptive school: A sourcebook for developing collaborative groups* (2nd ed.). Norwood, MA: Christopher-Gordon Publishers.

Gickling, E. E., Gravois, T. A., & Angell, V. (2016). *Instructional assessment: An essential path for guiding reading instruction*. Clearwater, FL: ICAT Publishing.

Gifford, K. (2012). What do you do when there are multiple concerns? Using problem identification to clarify and prioritize a teacher's concerns. In S. A. Rosenfield (Ed.), *Becoming a school consultant: Lessons learned* (pp. 85–98). New York: Routledge.

Glaser, J. E. (2014). *Conversational intelligence: How great leaders build trust and get extraordinary results*. Brookline, MA: Bibliomotion, Inc.

Gonsalvez, C. J., Brockman, R., & Hill, H. R. M. (2016). Video feedback in CBT supervision: Review and illustration of two specific techniques. *The Cognitive Behavior Therapist, 9*, 1–15.

Goodyear, R. K., Borders, L. D., Chang, C. Y., Guiffrida, D. A., Hutman, H., Kemer, G., Watkins, C., & White, E. (2016). Prioritizing questions and methods for an international and interdisciplinary supervision research agenda: Suggestions by eight scholars. *The Clinical Supervisor, 35*, 117–154

Gravois, T. A. (2013). Aligned service delivery: Ending the era of triage education. In L. C. Burrello, W. Sailor, & J. Kleinhammer-Tramill (Eds.), *Unifying educational systems: Leadership and policy perspectives* (pp. 109–134). New York: Taylor & Francis.

Gravois, T. A., Gickling, E. E., & Rosenfield, S. (2011). *Training in instructional consultation, assessment and teaming*. Catonsville, MD: ICAT Publishing.

Guiney, M. C., Harris, A., Zusho, A., & Cancelli, A. (2014). School psychologists' sense of self-efficacy for consultation. *Journal of Educational and Psychological Consultation, 24*, 28–54.

Guiney, M. C., & Zibulsky, J. (2016). Competent consultation: Developing self-efficacy for process and problem aspects of consultation. *Journal of Educational and Psychological Consultation, 27*, 52–71.

Gustafson, E. (2012). The importance of collaborative communication. In S. A. Rosenfield (Ed.), *Becoming a school consultant: Lessons learned* (pp. 73–84). New York: Routledge.

Gutkin, T. B., & Conoley, J. C. (1990). Reconceptualizing school psychology from a service delivery perspective: Implications for practice, training, and research. *Journal of School Psychology, 28*, 203–223.

Gutkin, T. B., & Curtis, M. J. (2009). School-based consultation: The science and practice of indirect service delivery. In T. B. Gutkin & C. R. Reynolds (Eds.), *Handbook of school psychology* (4th ed., pp. 591–635). New York: Wiley.

Guva, G. (2004). How to respond to teachers, who ask for help but not for consultation. In N. M. Lambert, I. Hylander, & J. H. Sandoval (Eds.), *Consultee-centered consultation:*

Improving the quality of professional services in schools and community organizations (pp. 255–264). Mahwah, NJ: Lawrence Erlbaum Associates.

Hackman, J. R., & Wageman, R. (2007). Asking the right questions about leadership: Discussion and conclusion. *American Psychologist, 62*, 43–47.

Hargreaves, A., & Fullan, M. (2012). *Professional capital: Transforming teaching in every school.* New York: Teachers College Press.

Harvey, V. S., & Struzziero, J. A., (2008). *Professional development and supervision of school psychologists: From intern to expert* (2nd ed.). Thousand Oaks, CA: Corwin Press.

Hatzichristou, C., Lampropoulou, A., Georgouleas, G., & Mihou, S. (2017). A multilevel approach to system-level consultation: Critical components and transnational considerations. In C. Hatzichristou & S. Rosenfield (Eds.), *The international handbook of consultation in educational settings* (pp. 70–93). New York: Routledge.

Hatzichristou, C., & Rosenfield, S. (Eds.). (2017). *The international handbook of consultation in educational settings.* New York: Routledge.

Hazel, C. E., Laviolette, G. T., & Lineman, J. M. (2010). Training professional psychologists in school-based consultation: What the syllabi suggest. *Training and Education in Professional Psychology, 4*, 235–243.

Hazel, C. E., Newman, D. S., & Barrett, C. A. (2016). Conducting rigorous survey research in the study of school-based consultation. *Journal of Educational and Psychological Consultation, 26*(2), 111–138.

Heckman-Stone, C. (2003). Trainee preferences for feedback and evaluation in clinical supervision. *The Clinical Supervisor, 22*(1), 21–23.

Higgins, E. T. (1999). "Saying is believing" effects: When sharing reality about something biases knowledge and evaluations. In L. L. Thompson, J. M. Levine, & D. M. Messick (Eds.), *Shared cognition in organizations: The management of knowledge* (pp. 33–49). Mahwah, NJ: Lawrence Erlbaum.

Hord, S. M. (2008). Evolution of the professional learning community: Revolutionary concept is based on intentional collegial learning. *Journal of Staff Development, 29*(3), 10–13.

Hosp, J. L., & Reschly, D. J. (2002). Regional differences in school psychology practice. *School Psychology Review, 31*, 11–29.

Huberman, M. (1993). The model of the independent artisan in teachers' professional relations. In J. W. Little & M. W. McLaughlin (Eds.), *Teachers' work: Individuals, colleagues and contexts* (pp. 11–50). New York: Teachers' College Press.

Hylander, I. (2004). Analysis of conceptual change in consultee-centered consultation. In N. M. Lambert, I. Hylander, & J. H. Sandoval (Eds.), *Consultee-centered consultation: Improving the quality of professional services in schools and community organizations* (pp. 45–61). Mahwah, NJ: Lawrence Erlbaum Associates.

Hylander, I. (2012). Conceptual change through consultee-centered consultation: A theoretical model. *Consulting Psychology Journal: Practice and Research, 64*, 29–45.

Hylander, I. (2017). Establishing psychological consultation services to promote student well-being in schools and preschools. In C. Hatzichristou & S. Rosenfield (Eds.), *The international handbook of consultation in educational settings* (pp. 15–34). New York: Routledge.

Illback, R. J. (2014). Organization development and change facilitation in school settings: Theoretical and empirical foundations. In W. P. Erchul & S. Sheridan (Eds.), *Handbook of research in school consultation* (2nd ed., pp. 276–303). New York: Routledge.

Ingraham, C. L. (2000). Consultation through a multicultural lens: Multicultural and crosscultural consultation in schools. *School Psychology Review, 29*, 320–343.

Ingraham, C. L. (2014). Studying multicultural aspects of consultation. In W. P. Erchul & S. Sheridan (Eds.), *Handbook of research in school consultation* (2nd ed., pp. 323–348). New York: Routledge.

Ingraham, C. L. (2017). Training and education of consultants. In C. Hatzichristou & S. Rosenfield (Eds.), *The international handbook of consultation in educational settings* (pp. 291–311). New York: Routledge.

Joyce, B., & Showers, B. (2002). *Student achievement through staff development* (3rd ed.). Alexandria, VA: ASCD.

Kaiser, L. T., Rosenfield, S., & Gravois, T. A. (2009). Teachers' perception of satisfaction, skill development, and skill application after instructional consultation services. *Journal of Learning Disabilities, 42,* 444–457.

Kaslow, N. J. (2004). Competencies in professional psychology. *American Psychologist, 59,* 774–781.

Kaslow, N. J., Grus, C. L., Campbell, L. F., Fouad, N. A., Hatcher, R. L., & Rodolfa, E. R. (2009). Competency assessment toolkit for professional psychology. *Training and Education in Professional Psychology, 3*(4)(Suppl.), S27–S45.

Kazdin, A. E. (2011). *Single case research designs: Methods for clinical and applied settings.* New York: Oxford University Press.

Kegan, R., & Lahey, L. L. (2001). *How the way we talk can change the way we work.* San Francisco: Jossey-Bass.

Kendall, P. C., & Beidas, R. S. (2007). Smoothing the trail for dissemination of evidence-based practices for youth: Flexibility within fidelity. *Professional Psychology: Research and Practice, 38,* 13–20.

Knotek, S. (2003). Bias in problem solving and the social process of student study teams: A qualitative investigation. *The Journal of Special Education, 37*(1), 2–14.

Kratochwill, T. R., Altschaefl, M. R., & Bice-Urbach, B. (2014). Best practices in school-based problem-solving consultation: Applications in prevention and intervention systems. In P. L. Harrison & A. Thomas (Eds.), *Best practices in school psychology: Data-based and collaborative decision making* (pp. 461–482). Bethesda, MD: National Association of School Psychologists.

Kratochwill, T. R., & Bergan, J. R. (1990). *Behavioral consultation in applied settings: An individual guide.* New York: Plenum Press.

Kratochwill, T. R., & Stoiber, K. C. (2002). Evidence-based interventions in school psychology: Conceptual foundations of the Procedural and Coding Manual of Division 16 and the Society for the Study of School Psychology Task Force. *School Psychology Quarterly, 17,* 341–389.

Kruse, S., Louis, K. S., & Bryk, A. (1994). Building professional community in schools. *Issues in restructuring schools, 6*(3), 67–71.

Laidley, D., Bambino, D., McIntyre, D., Quate, S., & Quinn, J. (2001). The paseo of circles of identity. In *National school reform faculty resource book.* Bloomington, IN: National School Reform Faculty.

Lambert, N. M., Hylander, I., & Sandoval, J. H. (Eds.). (2004). *Consultee-centered consultation: Improving the quality of professional services in schools and community organizations.* Mahwah, NJ: Lawrence Erlbaum Associates.

Little, J. W. (2007). Professional communication and collaboration. In W. D. Hawley & D. L. Rollie (Eds.), *The keys to effective schools: Education reform as a continuous improvement* (pp. 51–65). Thousand Oaks, CA: Corwin Press.

Lortie, D. C. (1975). *Schoolteacher: A sociological study.* Chicago: University of Chicago Press.

Lowman, R. L. (2015). Series editor forward. In J. Glover & H. L. Friedman (Eds.), *Transcultural competence: Navigating cultural differences in the global community* (pp. vii–x). Washington, DC: American Psychological Association.

Lowman, R. L., & Cooper, S. E. (2017). *The ethical practice of consulting psychology.* Washington, DC: American Psychological Association.

Maital, S. L. (2017). Thinking in the box: A tool for promoting innovative problem-solving in Israeli school psychology services. In C. Hatzichristou & S. Rosenfield (Eds.), *The international handbook of consultation in educational settings* (pp. 232–249). New York: Routledge.

Martens, B. K., DiGennaro Reed, F. D., & Magnuson, J. D. (2014). Behavioral consultation: Contemporary research and emerging challenges. In W. P. Erchul & S. Sheridan (Eds.), *Handbook of research in school consultation* (2nd ed., pp. 180–209). New York: Routledge.

Meyers, J., Meyers, A. B., & Grogg, K. (2004). Prevention through consultation: A model to guide future developments in the field of school psychology. *Journal of Educational and Psychological Consultation, 15,* 257–276.

Meyers, J., & Nastasi, B. (1999). Primary prevention in school settings. In C. Reynolds & T. Gutkin (Eds.), *Handbook of school psychology* (3rd ed., pp. 764–799). New York: Wiley.

Michelsen, E. (2004). Anger and gender in consultation. In N. M, Lambert, I. Hylander, & J. H. Sandoval (Eds.), *Consultee-centered consultation: Improving the quality of professional services in schools and community organizations* (pp. 291–299). Mahwah, NJ: Lawrence Erlbaum Associates Publishers.

Miller, G. A. (1969). Psychology as a means of promoting human welfare. *American Psychologist, 24,* 1063–1075.

Miranda, A. H. (Ed.). (2016). *Consultation across cultural contexts: Consultee-centered case studies.* New York: Routledge.

National Association of School Psychologists. (2010a). *Ethical and professional practices for school psychologists.* Bethesda, MD: Author.

National Association of School Psychologists. (2010b). *Standards for the graduate preparation of school psychologists.* Bethesda, MD: Author.

National Center for Education Statistics. (2016). *The condition of education 2016.* Retrieved from www.nces.ed.gov

Newell, M. L. (2012). Transforming knowledge to skill: Evaluating the consultation competence of novice school-based consultants. *Consulting Psychology Journal: Practice and Research, 64,* 8–28.

Newell, M. L., & Coffee, G. (2015). School psychologists as systems-level consultants: Interdisciplinary perspectives. *Journal of Educational & Psychological Consultation, 25,* 67–71.

Newman, D. S. (2012). Supervision of school-based consultation training: Addressing the concerns of novice consultants. In S. Rosenfield (Ed.), *Becoming a school consultant: Lessons learned* (pp. 49–70). New York: Routledge.

Newman, D. S. (2013). *Demystifying the school psychology internship.* New York: Routledge.

Newman, D. S., Barrett, C. A., & Hazel, C. E. (2015). School consultation practices in the early career: Does training matter? *Consulting Psychology Journal: Practice and Research, 67,* 326–347.

Newman, D. S., Hazel, C. E., Barrett, C. A., Chaudhuri, S. D., & Fetterman, H. (2017). Early career school psychologists' perceptions of consultative service delivery: The more things change, the more they stay the same. *Journal of Educational and Psychological Consultation.* Advanced online publication.

Newman, D. S., & Ingraham, C. (2017). Consultee-centered consultation: Contemporary perspectives and a framework for the future. *Journal of Educational and Psychological Consultation, 27*, 1–12.

Newman, D. S., McKenney, E., Silva, A. E., Clare, M., Salmon, D., & Jackson, S. (2017). A qualitative metasynthesis of school consultation process research: What we know and where to go. *Journal of Educational and Psychological Consultation, 27*, 13–51.

Newman, D. S., Salmon, D., Cavanaugh, K., & Schneider, M. F. (2014). The consulting role in a response-to-intervention context: An exploratory study of instructional consultation. *Journal of Applied School Psychology, 30*, 278–304.

Noell, G. H., Volz, J. R., Henderson, M.Y., & Williams, K. L. (2017). Evaluating an integrated support model for increasing treatment plan implementation following consultation in schools. *School Psychology Quarterly, 32*, 525–538.

O'Roark, A. M. (2002). Assessment and intervention issues in international organizational consulting. In R. L. Lowman (Ed.), *Handbook of organizational consulting psychology: Theory, skills, and techniques* (pp. 516–544). San Francisco: Jossey-Bass

Ortiz, S. O., & Melo, K. E. (2017). Foundations for consultation in educational settings with second language learners. In C. Hatzichristou & S. Rosenfield (Eds.), *The international handbook of consultation in educational settings* (pp. 137–159). New York: Routledge.

Pas, E. T. (2012). Case metamorphosis through consultation. In S. A. Rosenfield (Ed.), *Becoming a school consultant: Lessons learned* (pp. 195–209). New York: Routledge.

Pearson. (2013). *Pearson BOSS™ user's guide*. Retrieved from https://images.pearsonclinical.com/images/Assets/BOSS/BOSS_UsersGuide.pdf

Pickering, C. (2012). Relationship building and objectivity loss: The importance of the process in consultation. In S. A. Rosenfield (Ed.), *Becoming a school consultant: Lessons learned* (pp. 111–124). New York: Routledge.

Pluymert, K. (2014). Problem-solving foundations for psychological services. In P. L. Harrison & A. Thomas (Eds.), *Best practices in school psychology data-based and collaborative decision making* (pp. 25–39). Bethesda, MD: National Association of School Psychologists.

Pugach, M. C., Blanton, L. P., & Correa, V. I. (2011). A historical perspective on the role of collaboration in teacher education reform: Making good on the promise of teaching all students. *Teacher Education and Special Education, 34*(3), 183–200.

Quintero, E. (2017, Summer). Elevating relationships: How collaboration shapes teaching and learning. *American Educator, 41*(3), 18–21.

Reinke, W. M., Lewis-Palmer, T., & Merrell, K. (2008). The classroom check-up: A classwide teacher consultation model for increasing praise and decreasing disruptive behavior. *School Psychology Review, 37*, 315–332.

Reschly, A. L., & Reschly, D. J. (2014). School consultation and response to intervention: Convergence, divergence, and future directions for research and practice. In W. P. Erchul & S. Sheridan (Eds.), *Handbook of research in school consultation* (2nd ed., pp. 495–512). New York: Routledge.

Roediger III, H. L., Watson, J. M., McDermott, K. B., & Gallo, D. A. (2001). Factors that determine false recall: A multiple regression analysis. *Psychonomic Bulletin & Review, 8*, 385–407.

Rosenfield, S. A. (1987). *Instructional consultation*. Hillsdale, NJ: Erlbaum Associates.

Rosenfield, S. A. (1991). The relationship variable in behavioral consultation. *Journal of Behavioral Education, 1*, 329–336.

Rosenfield, S. A. (Ed.). (2012). *Becoming a school consultant: Lessons learned*. New York: Routledge.

Rosenfield, S. A. (2013). Consultation in the schools—are we there yet? *Consulting Psychology Journal: Practice and Research, 65*, 303–308.

Rosenfield, S. A. (2014). Best practices in instructional consultation and instructional consultation teams. In P. L. Harrison & A. Thomas (Eds.), *Best practices in school psychology: Data-based and collaborative decision making* (pp. 509–524). Bethesda, MD: National Association of School Psychologists.

Rosenfield, S. A., Gravois, T. A., & Silva, A. E. (2014). Bringing instructional consultation to scale: Research and development of IC and IC teams. In W. P. Erchul & S. Sheridan (Eds.), *Handbook of research in school consultation* (2nd ed., pp. 248–275). New York: Routledge.

Rosenfield, S. A., Levinsohn-Klyap, M., & Cramer, K. (2010). Educating consultants for practice in the schools. In E. Vasquez, T. Crespi, & C. Riccio (Eds.), *Handbook of education, training, and supervision of school psychologists in school and community* (Vol. 1, pp. 259–278). New York: Routledge.

Rosenfield, S. A., Newell, M., Zwolski, Jr., S., & Benishek, L. E. (2018). Evaluating problem-solving teams in k-12 schools: Do they work? *American Psychologist, 73*, 409–419.

Rosenfield, S. A., & Rubinson, F. (1985). Incorporating curriculum based assessment through consultation, *Exceptional Children, 52*, 282–287.

Rousmaniere, T., Goodyear, R. K., Miller, S. D., & Wampold, B. E. (Eds.). (2017). *The cycle of excellence: Using deliberate practice to improve supervision and training.* Hoboken, NJ: John Wiley & Sons.

Sander, J. B., Hernández Finch, M. E., & Newell, M. (2016). Introduction to special issue on multicultural competence in consultation. *Journal of Educational and Psychological Consultation, 26*, 213–219.

Sandoval, J. H. (2014). *An introduction to consultee-centered consultation in schools: A step-by-step guide in the process and skills.* New York: Routledge.

Sanetti, L. M. H., Fallon, L. M., & Collier-Meek, M. A. (2013). Increasing teacher treatment integrity through performance feedback provided by school personnel. *Psychology in the Schools, 50*, 134–150.

Sarason, S. B. (1971). *The culture of the school and the problem of change.* Boston: Allyn & Bacon.

Sarason, S. B. (1982). *The culture of the school and the problem of change* (2nd ed.). Boston: Allyn & Bacon.

Sarason, S. B. (1995). *School change: The personal development of a point of view.* New York: Teachers College Press.

Sarason, S. B. (1996). *Revisiting "The culture of the school and the problem of change."* New York: Teachers College Press.

Sarason, S. (2003/1966). Teaching as a lonely profession. In R. L. Fried (Ed.), *The skeptical visionary* (pp. 41–45). Philadelphia, PA: Temple University Press.

Sarason, S., Levine, M., Goldenberg, I., Cherlin, D., & Bennett, E. (1966). *Psychology in community settings: Clinical, educational, vocational, social aspects.* New York: Wiley.

Schein, E. H. (1999). *Process consultation revisited: Building the helping relationship.* Reading, MA: Addison-Wesley.

Schein, E. H. (2009). *Helping: How to offer, give, and receive help.* San Francisco: Berrett-Koehler.

Schein, E. H. (2013). *Humble inquiry: The gentle art of asking instead of telling.* San Francisco: Berrett-Koehler.

Schein, E. H. (2016). *Humble consulting: How to provide real help faster.* San Francisco: Berrett-Koehler.

Schon, D. A. (1983). *The reflective practitioner: How professionals think in action.* New York: Basic Books.

Schussler, L. (2012). Improving an English language learner client's comprehension through consultee-centered consultation. In S. A. Rosenfield (Ed.), *Becoming a school consultant: Lessons learned* (pp. 139–159). New York: Routledge.

Senge, P. M., Cambron-McCabe, N., Lucas, T., Smith, B., Dutton, J., & Kleiner, A. (2000). *Schools that learn: A fifth discipline fieldbook for educators, parents, and everyone who cares about education.* New York: Doubleday.

Senge, P. M., Kleiner, A., Roberts, C., Ross, R. B., & Smith, B. J. (1994). *The fifth discipline fieldbook: Strategies and tools for building a learning organization.* New York: Doubleday.

Sheridan, S. M., Clarke, B. L., & Christensen, S. L. (2014). Best practices in promoting family engagement in education. In P. Harrison & A. Thomas (Eds.), *Best practices in school psychology: Systems-level services* (pp. 439–453). Bethesda, MD: National Association of School Psychologists.

Sheridan, S. M., Clarke, B. L., & Ransom, K. A. (2014). The past, present, and future of conjoint behavioral consultation research. In W. P. Erchul & S. M. Sheridan (Eds.), *Handbook of research in school consultation* (2nd ed., pp. 210–247). New York: Erlbaum.

Sheridan, S. M., & Kratochwill, T. R. (2008). *Conjoint behavioral consultation: Promoting family-school connections and interventions* (2nd ed.). New York: Springer.

Sherry, E. (2012). Making the case for consultee-centered consultation: A novice consultant's perception of culture and relationships. In S. A. Rosenfield (Ed.), *Becoming a school consultant: Lessons learned* (pp. 99–109). New York: Routledge.

Silva, A. E., Newman, D. S., Guiney, M. C., Valley-Gray, S., & Barrett, C. A. (2016). Supervision and mentoring for early career school psychologists: Availability, access, structure, and implications. *Psychology in the Schools, 53*(5), 502–516.

Silverstein, S. (1974). *Where the sidewalk ends: The poems & drawings of Shel Silverstein.* New York: HarperCollins.

Simon, D. J. (2016). *School-centered interventions: Evidence-based strategies for social, emotional, and academic success.* Washington, DC: American Psychological Association.

Smith, J. (2017). *The use of brief functional analysis to reduce refusal behavior in a first-grade student with an autism spectrum disorder.* (Unpublished second year professional practice portfolio). University of Cincinnati, Cincinnati, OH.

Stoltenberg, C. D. (1993). Supervising consultants in training: An application of a model of supervision. *Journal of Counseling and Development, 72,* 131–138.

Stone, D., Patton, B., & Heen, S. (1999). *Difficult conversations: How to discuss what matters most.* New York: Penguin Books.

Stoner, G., & Green, S. (1992). Reconsidering the scientist-practitioner model for school psychology practice. *School Psychology Review, 21,* 155–167.

Tannen, D. (2007). *You just don't understand.* New York: William Morrow Paperbacks.

Tannen, D. (2017). *You're the only one I can tell: Inside the language of women's friendships.* New York: Ballantine Books.

Tarquin, K. A., & Truscott, S. D. (2006). Survey of school psychology students' perceptions of their practicum experiences. *Psychology in the Schools, 43,* 727–736.

Teachers and Parents as Partners. (2018). Retrieved from http://cyfs.unl.edu/TAPP/

Thomas, J. T. (2010). *The ethics of supervision and consultation: Practical guidance for mental health professionals.* Washington, DC: American Psychological Association.

Tindal, G., & Hasbrouck, J. (1991). Analyzing student writing to develop instruction strategies. *Learning Disabilities Research and Practice, 6,* 237–245.

Truscott, S. D., Cohen, C. E., Sams, D. P., Sanborn, K. J., & Frank, A. J. (2005). The current state(s) of prereferral intervention teams: A report from two national surveys. *Remedial and Special Education, 26*(3), 130–140.

Truscott, S. D., Kearney, M. A., Matthews, Y. T., & Daniel, K. (2017). Conducting school-based consultation as publishable research. In C. Hatzichristou & S. Rosenfield (Eds.), *The international handbook of consultation in educational settings* (pp. 357–377). New York: Routledge.

Tsakiris, E. (2012). Leaving no teacher behind: Widening the view and changing the perspective. In S. A. Rosenfield (Ed.), *Becoming a school consultant: Lessons learned* (pp. 211–231). New York: Routledge.

Vaganek, M. (2012). A teacher's concerns for one student reveals a classroom-wide bullying concern. In S. A. Rosenfield (Ed.), *Becoming a school consultant: Lessons learned* (pp. 177–192). New York: Routledge.

VanDerHeyden, A. M. (2014). Commentary: Evidence-based practice in school-based consultation research. In W. P. Erchul & S. Sheridan (Eds.), *Handbook of research in school consultation* (2nd ed., pp. 138–149). New York: Routledge.

Viswanathan, M., Golin, C. E., Jones, C. D., Ashok, M., Blalock, S. J., Wines, R. C., Coker-Schwimmer, E. J., Rosen, D. L., Sista, P., & Lohr, K. N. (2012). Interventions to improve adherence to self-administered medications for chronic diseases in the United States: A systematic review. *Annals of Internal Medicine, 157*, 785–795.

Vu, P., Bruckman Shanahan, K., Rosenfield, S., Gravois, T., Koehler, J., Kaiser, L., Berger, J., Vaganek, M., & Gottfredson, G. D (2013). Experimental evaluation of the effects of instructional consultation teams on teacher efficacy, instructional practices, collaboration, and job satisfaction. *International Journal of School and Educational Psychology, 1*, 67–81.

Walker, H. M., & Shinn, M. R. (2010). Systematic, evidence-based approaches for promoting positive student outcomes within a multi-tier framework: Moving from efficacy to effectiveness. In M. R. Shinn & H. M. Walker (Eds.), *Interventions for achievement and behavior problems in a three-tier model including RTI* (pp. 1–26). Washington, DC: National Association of School Psychologists.

Watzlawick, P. (1978). *The language of change: Elements of therapeutic communication.* New York: W. W. Norton & Co.

Wolf, M. M. (1978). Social validity: The case for subjective measurement or how applied behavior analysis is finding its heart. *Journal of Applied Behavior Analysis, 11*, 203–214.

Worrell, F. C., Naecker, J. E., Gerchow, C. E., Green, C., Kunesh, C. E., & Casey, A. (2017). Complicating the thinking of trainee consultants in consultee-centered consultation. In C. Hatzichristou & S. Rosenfield (Eds.), *The international handbook of consultation in educational settings* (pp. 332–354). New York: Routledge.

Wyner, N. B. (1991). Unlocking cultures of teaching: Working with diversity. In. N. B. Wyner (Ed.), *Current perspectives on the culture of schools* (pp. 95–107). Boston: Brookline Books.

Ysseldyke, J. E., Burns, M. K., Dawson, M., Kelly, B., Morrison, D., Ortiz, S., Rosenfield, S., & Telzrow, C. (2006). *School psychology: A blueprint for training and practice III.* Bethesda, MD: National Association of School Psychologists.

Ysseldyke, J. E., & Christenson, S. (2002). *Functional assessment of academic behavior: Creating successful learning environments.* Longmont, CO: Sopris West.

Zins, J. E., & Erchul, W. P. (2002). Best practices in school consultation. In A. Thomas & J. Grimes (Eds.), *Best practices in school psychology IV* (pp. 625–643). Bethesda, MD: NASP Publications.

INDEX